A Rough Guide to the

NEW TESTAMENT

DOWNLOADING
the Bible

Downloading the Bible: a rough guide to the New Testament

Copyright © 2000 by CWR Production P.O. Box 230, Farnham, Surrey, GU9 8XG, England.

Youth Specialties Books, 300 S. Pierce St., El Cajon, CA 92020, are published by Zondervan Publishing House, 5300 Patterson Ave. S.E., Grand Rapids, MI 49530.

Library of Congress Cataloging-in-Publication Data

Brant, Jonathan, 1970-
    Downloading the Bible : a rough guide to the New Testament
/ Jonathan Brant.
      p. cm.
    "Youth Specialties."
    ISBN 0-310-23426-3 (pbk. : alk. paper)
    1. Bible. N.T.–Introductions. I. Title.
  BS1475.2 .B64 2000
  223.6'1–dc21

                                        99-055173

Edited by Andrew Wooding and Vicki Newby
Cover and interior design by CWR Production and Razdezignz
Illustrations by David Yapp

Printed in the United States of America

00 01 02 03 04 05 06 /   / 10 9 8 7 6 5 4 3 2 1

A rough guide to the

NEW TESTAMENT

DOWNLOADING
the Bible

Jonathan **Brant**

Youth Specialties

CWR

ZondervanPublishingHouse
Grand Rapids, Michigan
A Division of HarperCollinsPublishers

CONTENTS

List of features included in this book

WHY SHOULD I WASTE MY VALUABLE TIME READING THIS BOOK?

wash hair

Do you have cable TV or a satellite dish? At first it's so exciting: "Oh boy! There are 24 hours a day of Hungarian soaps on channel 307 and a nail-bitingly exciting armadillo-tossing contest on the sports channel!"

Soon, though, you come to realize the really good programs are on premium channels, and you have to pay extra for a decoder if you want to watch them.

I once lived with a family who had cable TV, and sometimes, when I became bored with the armadillo toss, I would try to watch the special channels. Even without a decoder it was almost possible to tell what's going on.

"Yep, that's definitely basketball. Oh, no wait, it could be the new Eddie Murphy film." Occasionally there's even a moment of total and beautiful clarity: "That's not Eddie Murphy—it's the Queen of England!"

But generally I was peering through a thick fog, the characters' feet at the top of the screen, their heads at the bottom, and thick wavy lines running all through the middle. A less than satisfying viewing experience.

Unfortunately, reading the Bible can be a lot like watching cable TV without a decoder. The story, or the teaching, seems to appear and disappear through a thick fog. We think we know what's going on, but to be honest we're not quite sure. The characters seem upside down and incomprehensible, and what on earth does all this have to do with us anyway?

Still, we plow on (if we have the strength), waiting for that one moment of beautiful clarity when God speaks to us through a particular word or verse—then we plunge back into the fog. Nobody wants that.

So, we present this little book—our version of a decoder—to help you tune in when you read the Bible.

But why should I need a decoder?

Maybe you're saying, "But if the Bible is God's Word, won't the Holy Spirit decode it for me? Why do I need a book to help?"

It's a fair question. There are moments of total, beautiful clarity, no doubt. But God also expects us to expend a little effort ourselves. That's part of God's plan for us.

Here's something to think about. If you traveled back in time just 10 years ago, when I was in school, much of the playground conversation would be completely unintelligible.

Think of slang—would you be insulted or pleased to be called an "Alpha Geek" or a "Mod"? What about TV programs—could you discuss the plot of "Dallas" or laugh at jokes about the Fonz in "Happy Days"? Was "Adam Ant" a kiddie creation like Scooby Doo or a famous singer?

Even in the space of 10 years, people's lifestyles and interests change significantly. So it's interesting to remember the most recent parts of the Bible were written *2,000* years ago. But don't worry. God is not disconnected from all this. God made sure that even though it was written in different languages from ours, by people who never dreamt of cars or factories—let alone computers, modems, or space travel—we can still understand much of what the Bible is about. With a little effort, we can understand *much* more.

It's particularly useful to know how the people of the Bible lived, what they liked and disliked, what they cared about, and what scared them.

And once we know something about when and why a particular book of the Bible was written, what we read will make much more sense.

So, whadaya think? Is it worth the effort to understand? Read on…

So how do I use this book, anyway?

I had a friend who was a genius at math and science but dumb as dirt in English. He failed English three times. We'll never know if he really passed or if they just took pity and let him slide.

One reason he kept failing was he insisted his best chance of getting through was to memorize whole chunks from *Cliffs Notes*. When he walked into an exam, his brain was bursting with a memorized beginning and ending of a story (he just had to fill in the middle). It never occurred to him his teacher might be clever enough to recognize *Cliffs Notes,* or that—call me crazy—it would a better use of his time to just sit down and *read* one of the books.

Sure, fine, make fun of my friend. But understand this: his approach to learning English wasn't much different from the way a lot of people approach the Bible. We like Bible study books but don't get around to actually reading the Bible. Maybe that's slightly better than nothing. But wouldn't it be ever so slightly better to go straight to the source?

Some things were just made to go together: Big Macs and fries, Tom and Jerry, this book and the Bible! Ideally, you should read with this book in one hand and the Bible in the other. The whole idea is to help you understand the Bible better and learn more about what God is saying through it as you read.

Actually, it's a two-way street. You can start by reading the Bible and then come here for more background information. Or you can drive in the other direction, starting with this book and then looking up the parts it recommends in the Bible.

The components of this book

Each book of the New Testament is covered in *this* book, so whatever book you are reading you should be able to look it up in the Contents and turn directly to the right page to find the information you want.

For simplicity, the books are covered here in the same order they appear in your Bible.

Most books are dealt with in groups that make them easier to understand. The Gospels are all together, as are the letters written by the Apostle Paul.

The sections often include some general background information. It might be worth taking a look at these to get an idea of the kind of books you are reading.

Once you reach the explanations about individual books, you will find a number of paragraphs with different headings. Here is what you will find—

Like the blurb on the back of a book or a video, the first few paragraphs are intended to give you an idea of what the book is about and catch your interest so you'll want to read on.

The next several sections cover questions like these: Who wrote this book and when? Who was it written for? Why was it written? This information is there to help you understand the message of the book.

Main theme

If you've read the Bible quite often you'll know that sometimes it's almost impossible to see the wood for the trees. You think, "But what on earth does this mean? Why is this story here at all?" Some of the books are so long and cover so many different stories and topics that it's impossible to guess at what the overall message is.

This section attempts to sum up what we might learn from the book as a whole if we had the time and energy to read it from cover to cover in one shot.

You can then keep this in mind as you read bits of it and see where individual stories fit into the overall message.

a long book of the Bible

Interesting bits
and
Other interesting bits

This is possibly the most important and helpful information of all, because it will help you to pick up the Bible and explore new territory. These lists should lead you through the minefield of difficult or confusing parts into the heart of the Bible book you're reading. If there's a person that you're especially interested in or a story that you particularly want to read, you should find it here.

Many of the passages listed here are the bits that are underlined in my own Bible—the parts I have found interesting in the past. They're just a taste and won't include everything in the book that's important and exciting. As you read more you could add your own **Interesting bits** to the list.

The far-out side

If it's all getting to be a bit much, here are a few paragraphs that explore the outer limits of what is recorded in the Bible in a more lighthearted way.

A few clues about reading the Bible

Little and often

Some restaurants advertise the fact that if you can eat your way through the entire menu, you eat for free. For snakes (which can eat one huge meal and then digest it for weeks afterward) that would be a cheap way to live—slither in once a month, and then slide (rather slowly) home to digest all that free food. But that's not how we humans work. We must eat a little and often.

It's the same with Bible reading. What we need is to dip into the Bible as often as possible but not wear ourselves out by doing too much at once. Why not set modest goals for reading the Bible and see what God might do to help you meet them? Don't worry if you don't stick to your plans perfectly; slow and steady wins the race. Try to keep going—or try something fresh if what you're doing isn't working. Do anything—just don't stop!

Read past, present, and future

I want to recommend a time traveler's way of reading the Bible that will make it easier to understand and apply to your life. When you read a few verses in the Bible and want to know what they mean to you, try this approach.

Past—Ask yourself questions about when the verses were originally written. Who wrote them and why? Who were they written for and why? You will find this information in this book.

Present—Next, ask yourself what the verses could mean to you today.

Future—Finally, ask yourself: 'What am I going to do or think differently in the future in the light of what these verses of the Bible say to me?'

Reading the Bible this way invites God to speak to us and, more importantly, puts us in a position to act on what we hear God saying!

eat your way thru the menu for free!

MENU

Deuteronomy Joshua Judges Ruth 1 Samu
overbs Ecclesiastes Song of Songs Isaiah
iah Jonah Micah Nahum Habakkuk Zephan
Romans 1 Corinthians
2 Timothy Titus Philer
2 Corinthians Galatians Ephesians Philip
on Hebrews James 1 Peter 2 Peter 1 John

The

HOLY
BIBLE

NEW INTERNATIONAL VERSION

Containing the Old Testament
and the New Testament

WHAT'S SO SPECIAL ABOUT THE BIBLE?

2 Samuel 1 Kings 2 Kings
Jeremiah Lamentations Ezekiel
Haggai Zechariah Malachi

2 Corinthians Galatians Ephesians Philipp
on Hebrews James 1 Peter 2 Peter 1 John

ans Colossians 1 Thessalonians
2 John 3 John Jude Revelation

What's so special about the Bible?

Danger: Creative genius at work!

Can you imagine living in a monochromatic world? A universe with only one color?

Fortunately, the God who created the universe is a genius. Our world is not black and white but an incredible, multicolor paradise. The latest computer printers and monitors claim to be able to reproduce millions of colors. Impressive—but only a fraction of the colors God used to paint the world.

God went wild! Like some sort of mad professor, he was never content with just doing the job—it had to be fantastic, beautiful, outrageous, and extreme.

Just think of all the different tastes, different animals, different landscapes, different smells—and compare Adam Sandler with Neve Campbell. The world is full of the weird and the wonderful!

Let me introduce myself

Just imagine that the incredible, creative genius wanted to tell you about himself and give you some clues about his creation—your home planet. Imagine he decided to communicate to you through a book. Would he write a boring book?

Not! The Bible, God's most specific and detailed way of revealing himself to us, is like the world we live in: a work of genius.

What will I find in the Bible?

The Bible is chock-full of the mysterious and the bizarre.

If the FBI had been around when the Bible was being written, Mulder and Scully would have been run ragged investigating X-file after X-file: a talking donkey, a disembodied finger appearing to write cryptic graffiti on the wall at a king's banquet, and the awesome teacher and prophet who turned water to wine and multiplied a kid's lunch to feed thousands.

But it's not all the stuff of tabloid news headlines. The Bible tells epic tales of war and bloodthirsty battle. Romantic heroes are everywhere: a brave boy defeats a terrible giant, wise leaders save their countries from destruction, beautiful women risk everything to change the course of history, true friends risk their lives to help each other.

But there is a problem

As you read this you might be thinking, "Well, if the Bible is so popular and so exciting, how come I find it so hard to read and understand?"

Fair question. The truth is, the Bible is far more exciting and interesting than a simple textbook, but it takes more effort to understand. Like most things, the more you put in, the more you get out. As any football lover knows, winning seasons require careful planning and disciplined effort—just passing a ball around won't cut it. In the same way we need to find out something about the background of the various parts of the Bible to fully understand and enjoy it.

Turn the page for basic information about the Bible as a whole.

The X Files

That big black book on your shelf

If you were to pull down a Bible from your shelf, you'd find it's not just a continuous stream of words—which is good because, taken together, it's one long, long book. There are over 750,000 words, which is equal to more than 20 ordinary novels. I'm happy to report the Bible is divided very sensibly.

The first and biggest division is between the two **testaments**. As you probably know these are called the **Old Testament** and the **New Testament**. The word *testament* means agreement or relationship.

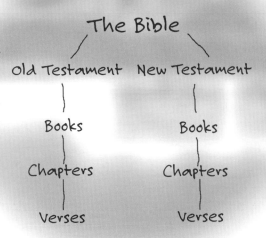

The Old Testament is about the agreement that God made with the ancient nation of Israel.

The New Testament is about the fresh agreement God made with all people through Jesus Christ.

Each testament is then broken down into separate **books**—39 in the old and 27 in the new.

There are two more divisions, which make it much easier to find particular sections. They are the divisions of the books into **chapters** and **verses**. These weren't put there by the authors—they were added much later when people began to print the Bible in large numbers.

But who wrote all those books?

If God ran an employment agency, it's safe to say he would hire some interesting people. God obviously has his own ideas about what qualifies someone to do a certain job. I imagine if we wanted someone to write books for us, we would probably choose people with degrees in English or journalism.

But the people God "employed" to write his book were from all different walks of life. Some, like Moses and Paul, were highly educated scholars. Some were professionally religious—priests and prophets like Jeremiah and Ezekiel. Still others were normal, working folk: fishermen like Peter, doctors like Luke, farmers like Amos. God even chose a couple of kings, David and Solomon, to have a hand in writing his book.

So it's not really God's book at all then?

Some things in life will always remain mysteries. Why are dinosaurs extinct? Why do we suffer some form of instantaneous brain freeze when we try to make small talk with desirable members of the opposite sex? And how, exactly, did God inspire the writers of the Bible?

We'll probably never understand. Second Timothy 3:16 declares that God was involved in its writing, saying, "All Scripture is God-breathed"—but that doesn't help much on the *how* front.

One thing we do know: it wasn't some sort of divine dictation. God used the particular personalities, experiences, and situations of each of the writers to make their books unique. God guided each of them in such a way that each one revealed an important part about God's character and plans and about the way God works in the world.

So it's absolutely correct to think of the Bible as God's Word to us. Because, miraculously, it is.

Types and styles of writing

There are many different types of writing in the Bible. To impress an English teacher, you might call them *genres* of writing. For example—

History—where the deeds of kings and the political experiences of the nation of Israel are recorded.

Proverbs—where wise advice is stated in short, unforgettable, sometimes funny, sayings.

Poetry—almost everyone can quote at least a line or two from the poem-psalm that begins, "The Lord is my shepherd."

Biography—where the words and actions of Jesus are recorded by people who knew him face-to-face and heard his teaching with their own ears.

Songs—songs of love in the Song of Songs, which contains the unbeatable line, "Your teeth are white like newly sheared sheep just coming in from their bath"; and songs of praise to God, some of which we still sing today.

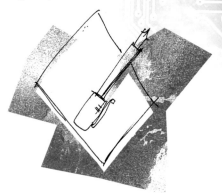

But is it true?

Imagine a tough New York cop interviewing witnesses to a bank robbery. If every witness walked into the office, sat down, and described what happened in exactly the same words as the others, the policeman would begin to suspect a conspiracy. It simply doesn't work that way. Honest witnesses will argue over the color of the getaway car, the height of the robber, and particularly the order in which things happened. After all, they are human beings, not video cameras. The police expect such differences. No criminal would ever be convicted if witnesses were considered unreliable because of different recollections of this sort.

It's precisely the same with the Bible. The very few and small disagreements over minor facts (opponents of the Bible love to point them out) just serve to prove the Bible isn't a hoax—it hasn't been carefully altered to make it look more reliable.

The big issues

Consider these issues: the origin of the universe, whether God exists, the problem of human good and evil, the question of

what happens when we die...

If you were to discuss those issues in class, or even among friends, you could expect huge arguments. Billy thinks we've all descended from spacemen. Mary is convinced humans are basically good because her baby niece is so sweet. Alfred, the scientist, reckons we're just animals.

Yet all the authors of the Bible are in perfect agreement about these issues and many more equally complex ones. Add to this the fact that no archaeological dig ever discovered anything that disproves the history of the Bible, and you should begin to have more than enough evidence to conclude the Bible is true.

But there is more—changed lives

The best evidence that the Bible is truly God's book is its powerful effect on people's lives. Many, many people have been converted to Christianity simply by reading the Bible. It has the startling property of suddenly coming alive in the minds of people who read it and totally changing their lifelong thoughts and understanding about life.

Whoa, big issues

THE BIBLE

Big issues (Sunday editions of the New York Times)

It's because of this that there are millions of people on the planet who consider the Bible their most treasured possession. Risks are taken each day to smuggle Bibles into closed societies. The reason for the risk is that Christians living in those countries are so desperate for God's Word. No other book has quite that effect on people.

No other book is God's Word

John

The Word Became Flesh

1 In the beginning was the Word, and the Word was with God, and the Word was God. [2] He was with God in the beginning. [3] Through him all things were made; without him nothing was made that has been made. [4] In him was life, and that life was the light of men. [5] The light shines in the darkness, but the darkness has not understood it.

[6] There came a man who was sent from God; his name was John. [7] He came as a witness to testify concerning that light, so that through him all men might believe. [8] He himself was not the light; he came only as a witness to the light. [9] The true light that gives light to every man was coming into the world.

[10] He was in the world, and though the world was made through him, the world did not recognize him. [11] He came to that which was his own, but his own did not receive him. [12] Yet to all who received him, to those who believed in his name, he gave the right to become children of God— [13] children born not of natural descent, nor of human decision or a husband's will, but born of God. [14] The Word became flesh and made his dwelling among us. We have seen his glory,

[15] John testifies concerning him.

John the Baptist Denies Being the Christ

[19] Now this was John's testimony when the Jews of Jerusalem sent priests and Levites to ask him who he was. [20] He did not fail to confess, but confessed freely, "I am not the Christ."

[21] They asked him, "Then who are you? Are you Elijah?"

He said, "I am not."

"Are you the Prophet?"

He answered, "No."

[22] Finally they said, "Who are you? Give us an answer to take back to those who sent us. What do you say about yourself?"

[23] John replied in the words of Isaiah the prophet, "I am the voice of one calling in the desert, 'Make straight the way for the Lord.'"

[24] Now some Pharisees who had been sent [25] questioned him, "Why then do you baptize if you are not the Christ, nor Elijah, nor the Prophet?"

[26] "I baptize with water," John replied, "but among you stands one you do not know. [27] He is the one who comes after me, the thongs of whose sandals I am not worthy to untie."

[28] This all happened at Bethany on the other side of the Jordan, where John was baptizing.

Jesus the Lamb of God

[29] The next day John saw Jesus coming toward him and said, "Look, the Lamb of God, who takes away the sin of the world!

THE NEW TESTAMENT

Downloading

Matthew
Mark
Luke
John
Acts
Romans
1 Corinthians
2 Corinthians
Galatians
Ephesians
Philippians
Colossians
1 Thessalonians
2 Thessalonians
1 Timothy
2 Timothy
Titus
Philemon
Hebrews
James
1 Peter
2 Peter
1 John
2 John
3 John
Jude
Revelation

THE WORLD of the NEW TESTAMENT

hew Mark Luke John Acts Roman
Matthew Mark Luke John Acts
1 Thessalonians 2 Thessaloni
hessalonians 2 Thessalonians

Downloading

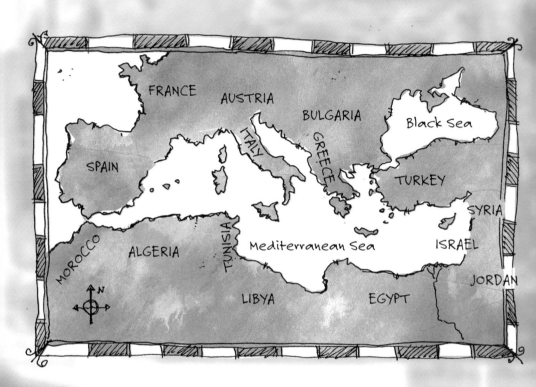

SOME MODERN MEDITERRANEAN NATIONS IN THE EARLY 21ST CENTURY

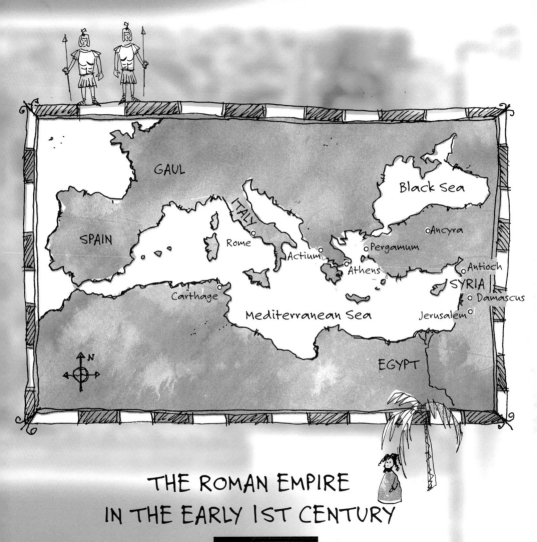

GAUL

SPAIN

ITALY

Rome

Actium

Athens

Carthage

Black Sea

Ancyra

Pergamum

Antioch

SYRIA

Damascus

Jerusalem

Mediterranean Sea

EGYPT

N

THE ROMAN EMPIRE
IN THE EARLY 1ST CENTURY

Romans and Greeks (the Gentiles)

Luxury for a few, squalor for most

What's the biggest risk you've ever taken? Eating your sister's cooking class project? Or staying in the room when your brother takes off his cross-trainers?

In Roman times, just being born was a huge gamble. A happy or a terrible life depended on the coincidence of being born a boy or a girl, rich or poor. The rich lived in huge mansions with running water, gardens, and heating. But the poorest people lived in multistory apartment blocks that were a real health hazard—they kept falling down! And you had to learn to keep your legs crossed because they certainly didn't have indoor plumbing.

Girls weren't popular and were often left outside to die as soon as they were born. Some of these unwanted babies were picked up by slave traders and ended up as prostitutes or priestesses in pagan temples.

What did they eat?

Forget three square meals. Romans ate at least four times a day.

On the downside, the diet wasn't quite as varied as it might have been. Out: fast food, chips, chocolate, and soft drinks. In: lentils, goats' milk, olives, bacon, fish, sausage, and diluted wine.

What did they wear?

Nice legs

Nice legs, mister! Both men and women wore a short tunic that exposed their legs from about the knee down. This tunic was usually white, and women sometimes wore a much longer, brighter one on top. In cold weather, men and women covered their tunic with a thick cloak.

It was common for both sexes to dye their hair, curl it, and plaster it down with oil and perfume—not to mention wearing wigs and hair extensions. Women, and some men, also used huge quantities of makeup and wore lots of jewels, including earrings and nose rings. Pretty much the natural look, really. Is it just me, or have you seen modern Romans hanging out at the mall?

What about Friday nights?

It's Friday night. You've got a good-looking date and money in your pocket, but where to go? Without Hollywood to keep them amused, the Greeks and Romans came up with their own entertainment.

The Olympic Games and chariot racing were big sporting events, but nothing could match the spectacle and adrenaline of the amphitheater. Shows in these vast arenas were often gore fests—gladiators fought to the death, ferocious wild animals slaughtered each other, and so much blood was spilled that the saturated sand had to be replaced several times per show!

Other pastimes were equally X-rated: prostitution was common and pornographic pictures covered the walls of public places. Divorce was easy and frequent, and affairs and violent crimes were common. Déjà vu.

Campus life

Boys were first educated by a family slave; then they continued at a major university somewhere like Athens or Rhodes. Girls were prevented from going to school.

"Wait a minute," I hear you cry. "What could be cruel about letting me skip school?"

Well, it stopped girls from becoming educated and living as full a life as boys were able to live. Doesn't that seem cruel?

At work

If you visited a career counselor in those times, he might recommend many jobs still popular today. There were bankers, retail clerks, farmers, sailors, soldiers, even dentists and doctors.

Dentists could fill your teeth with gold or give you false teeth made from teeth pulled from a dead person's mouth (lovely thought).

Ancient doctors needed one qualification above all others—determination. You had to be able to continue with your operation in spite of screams and pleas for mercy from your unsedated patient. Yikes!

The Religious World of the Gentiles

Greek deities on Olympus

The Greeks invented a complicated family of gods and goddesses whom they worshiped.

The top job went to Zeus who ruled from Mount Olympus. The gods he ruled were immortal and incredibly powerful, but otherwise behaved like naughty schoolchildren—always stealing, arguing, and fighting.

There were many temples to these gods in ancient cities. Priests, priestesses, and prophets tried to guide the people in their attempts to communicate with the gods.

Roman versions of Greek gods

The Romans took the Greek gods and gave them Roman names. Few people really trusted or wholly believed in these unlikable gods, but they kept up the pretense of worshiping them, perhaps because they were scared. If the gods were known for anything, it was for their cruelty to humans who displeased them.

Dead Roman emperors were also thought of as gods, and certain living emperors began to demand that people worship and pray to them as well. This caused Christians lots of problems because their refusal to worship the emperor was considered rebellion.

Mystery religions

Did you ever have a secret club with hand signs, code language, and secret meeting places?

Secret religious clubs were very popular in Roman times. Because they were so—well, secret, we really don't know much about what they believed. What we do know is they had special signs and handshakes for recognizing each other, and you had to swear bloodthirsty oaths of secrecy to become a member—you probably didn't have that last part in your childhood club.

Superstition

Forget the horoscope in the back of your favorite magazine. The Greeks and Romans had many more weird ways of

Greek God   Geek God

predicting the future.

They did follow the stars and horoscopes, but they also watched the flight of birds, poured oil onto water and watched the way it moved, and split open dead animals to see in what order their guts fell out. Yuck!

They also believed in magic and demons, and people made lots of money selling spells or special charms and doing weird dances or ceremonies to chase off evil spirits.

Popular philosophies of the 1st century

Apart from religion, there were many other views on how to live your life. These are some of the more popular:

Gnostics—They thought the body was evil but the soul was good.

Epicureans—For these guys, pleasure was the name of the game: get some if you can.

Stoics—These tough guys taught that winning the lottery or losing a loved one should be greeted with the same amount of emotion—none.

Cynics—Self-control is the highest virtue, and being influenced by others is a weakness.

Skeptics—They doubted everything and believed in nothing.

Why Jesus made sense

Few of the millions of people in the Roman Empire followed either a particular religion or a particular philosophy. Most were simply superstitious. Religiously, they lived in a frightening fog where hideous shapes appeared and disappeared, cruel gods played wicked games with their lives, and nobody seemed to be able to make sense of it for them.

This meant many were open to Christianity when it came because it offered a loving and caring God and answers to the questions of the universe.

The World of the Jews

Togetherness!

Jewish families tended to be large and much closer (literally) than the Romans and Greeks. You could forget about getting your own bedroom. The average family—and their animals—all slept in one room. (At least there were plenty of other suspects if the baked beans you ate for dinner had their usual effect.)

Sadly, sexism existed in Jewish families, too. The birth of a baby boy caused great rejoicing, while the birth of a girl was considered a disappointment. If a Jewish family member died, the extended family wailed, tore their clothes, and perhaps even paid professional mourners to come in and do the job properly. Too bad they didn't treat the living as well.

What to eat?

Most people have some idea of what the Jews were not allowed to eat—a café owner in Jerusalem would be unlikely to do big business in ham sandwiches—but what *did* they eat?

Most Jewish people lived off bread, fruit, and vegetables—meat was only for special occasions. Since sugar was unknown (*was life worth living?* we ask ourselves), they used raisins, figs, or honey as sweeteners. They also ate a lot of fish, and this kept at least some of Jesus' disciples in business.

Synagogue school

Young Jewish children were given a very basic education by their parents—in Jewish history and religion and in practical skills like potty training and mud pies.

Around the age of six, the boys would go on to the synagogue schools. Here the Old Testament was the textbook for math ("Count the words in the book of Joshua") and history (that's Old Testament history and biology—"Now, when King David saw Bathsheba in the bath…").

All Jewish boys were also taught a trade. Remember, Jesus was trained as a carpenter.

If you wanted more schooling (it happens, you know), you found an older rabbi or teacher and became his personal pupil.

What about the girls? Well, when it came to education, the girls might as well have been Gentiles.

Hi-ho, hi-ho, it's off to work we go

Most Jewish men followed the trade they were trained in as boys. Fishermen, farmers, shopkeepers, and carpenters were common.

Tax collectors, not so much. If you liked being called names and spit at every time you walked out your door, you could become a tax collector. The Jews hated the fact that the Romans were in control of their country. And they hated any of their countrymen who made a profit by collaborating with the Romans—like, tax collectors, for example. This is why people were shocked when Jesus ate, or even spoke, with tax collectors.

Love and marriage

Frightening thought—what if your parents got to pick the person you were to marry? ("But, Dad, she has to shave more often than I do!") That's exactly what happened to young Jewish men and women.

It does seem the would-be bride and groom had some opportunity to protest, but this would probably be severely frowned upon by the rest of the family. So you had to hope your mom and dad had good taste!

Boyfriend-girlfriend relationships were unheard of. Many girls would have been married or at least betrothed (a strict engagement) by the time they were teenagers, so there wasn't much time for tongue-tangles behind the gym.

This explains the Bible's lack of advice on this sort of relationship (I'm thinking a brief exposition on the difference between a holy and an unholy kiss would be useful, but maybe that's just me).

Jewish Religious Life

Every school has the sort of macho mouth who talks like Clint Eastwood when 10 of his friends are around, yet turns into Mr. Rogers when he's on his own. That was the way with the Greek gods—such a sorry bunch that there had to be loads of them.

The Jews needed only one God—the Almighty YAHWEH (that's *Mister* Yah-way to you, bub). His history with them as his chosen people is recorded in their sacred book—what Christians call the Old Testament.

Mistaken identity

Have you ever built up a picture in your mind of what someone must be like, and then you meet her and she's totally different?

The Jews were waiting for a Messiah sent by God, but when Jesus turned up, most didn't recognize him. They were looking for someone completely different—a brilliant general who would throw out the Romans or a brilliant king to rule on earth forever. They didn't expect God himself to slip in the back door in human form, they didn't expect him to be born to a virgin, they didn't expect him to die, and they were freaked out by the claim that he rose from the dead.

The synagogue

Big, thick Swiss Army knives are cool. I bet in a few years' time there will be a blade that pops up and becomes a mobile phone, and one that tells you the answers to your math homework.

The synagogue was the Swiss Army knife of the Jewish life and the center of each Jewish community. The boys' school was only one of its many functions.

The simple, rectangular room had a raised platform at one end and a big chest, which contained the valuable Old Testament scrolls. The synagogue was a church on Sabbath days. Other days it was a funeral home, a help center for the poor, a place for political meetings, or a court for Jewish law (the synagogue elders could even give punishment by whipping, a power some church leaders today might appreciate).

The temple

While there were many synagogues, there was only one temple—a huge, magnificent building in the city of Jerusalem.

Gentile tourists could enter the outer parts of the temple, but there were huge signs in different languages forbidding anyone but Jews to enter the inner courts—on pain of death. It was in the temple that the animal sacrifices were made by the priests.

A Who's Who of Jewish groups

This is a quick guide to some of the Jewish religious groups you might meet as you read the New Testament.

Pharisees—Some of these guys were probably well-intentioned, but on the whole they don't look so good when we read the New Testament. They tried their best to keep the Old Testament law, but took things a little too far: "Don't spit on the ground on the Sabbath, because the dirt might move and that's practically plowing, which is forbidden." They had also become proud of themselves and looked down on other people. That really got Jesus' goat.

Jesus' goat

Sadducees—Many of the priests who worked in the temple were Sadducees. They grew rich by working closely with the Romans, and they didn't believe in life after death, angels, demons, or anything as primitive as that.

Scribes—This term really describes the profession of these men. They were part lawyer, part teacher, part professional secretary. They taught and interpreted the Law God gave to the Jews in the Old Testament.

Sanhedrin—Before his crucifixion, Jesus was tried in front of the Sanhedrin. It was the highest court of the Jews and included members of all of the groups named above.

Here a Jew, there a Jew, everywhere I go a Jew

I'm always surprised to run into a Colorado Rockies fan in New York City or a Utah Jazz fan in Chicago. The truth is that people live wherever they live and like whichever team they like.

It was the same with the Jewish people. There were probably about four million of them in the Roman Empire, but fewer than a quarter of these actually lived in Israel. Instead, they were spread out through all the cities of the Empire.

The Four Gospels

Matthew Mark
Luke John

Acts

Romans 1 Corinthia
2 Corinthians Galatia
Philippians Colossia
2 Thessalonians 1
2 Timothy Titus

The Acts of the Apostles

Paul's Letters

Other Letters

Ephesians
1 Thessalonians
mothy
ilemon

Hebrews James
1 Peter 2 Peter
1 John 2 John 3 John
Jude

Revelation

Revelation

The Four Gospels

Two thousand years ago the world was rocked to its very core. Not by a meteor or something else from outer space, but by a man—Jesus of Nazareth. He split world history in two. Before his birth, B.C.—after, A.D., anno Domini, the year of the Lord. We can meet him in the four Gospels.

Definition of *gospel*

Imagine living in an ancient city at war. Every morning you wake up in fear of invading enemy soldiers stealing, raping, and murdering. If a messenger arrived saying your side had won and you were free, it would be good news, wouldn't it?

Well, that kind of good news is what the word *gospel* originally meant. In time it was attached to the four books written about Jesus' life—because they told the good news of the battle he won for us.

Why were the Gospels written?

The apostles, who knew and lived with Jesus, became increasingly important—like human hard drives full of information about him. But unfortunately they began to die. The race was on to record all they knew about Jesus' life before it was too late. God inspired some of them—and other writers working with them—to write the Gospels.

But why are there four?

Have you noticed that all designers, from civil engineers to artistic fashion students, now work on computers? The big advantage is it's now possible to work not just in two dimensions, like on paper, but in three—like the real world. A 3-D image on a computer can be turned around and viewed from every side.

If God inspired only one author to write one account of Jesus, it would have been very useful—but one dimensional. Since we have four, all looking at Jesus from a slightly different angle, it's like seeing him in three—or even four—dimensions.

How are they related?

If Matthew, Mark, and Luke had placed their three essays in front of an English teacher, there would have been big trouble and some accusations of cheating flying around.

It's generally believed Mark was written first and that Matthew and Luke used his Gospel as the basis for the flow of action in their accounts. In some places they blatantly copied.

It was a common and acceptable practice to quote a reliable source, as it is today in news organizations. It doesn't discount their historical accuracy or make God's inspiration and involvement any less.

A life of Jesus

If you tried to write a sort of music fanzine article about Jesus, it would be pretty boring. For a star, there are no photos of him available.

Today, we like to know absolutely everything about famous people—from the color of their boxer shorts to their favorite brand of deodorant, and with whom they enjoyed their first kiss.

It wasn't the same when Jesus was around. Although his life is better documented than any other ancient person, we still don't know much about the personal details. If we put together the main things we know, the chart would look like the one on page 41.

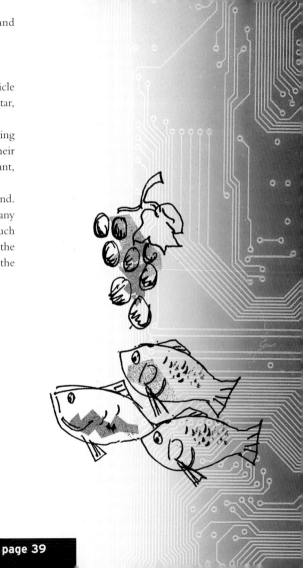

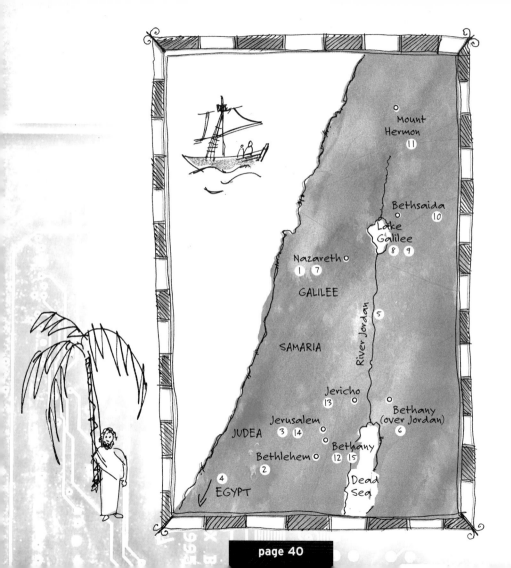

Mount Hermon
11

Bethsaida
10

Lake Galilee
8 9

Nazareth
1 7

GALILEE

River Jordan
5

SAMARIA

Jericho
13

Bethany (over Jordan)
6

Jerusalem
3 14

JUDEA

Bethany
12 15

Bethlehem
2

EGYPT

Dead Sea

EVENTS OF JESUS' LIFE

1 Announcement of birth

2 Birth

3 Presentation in the temple

4 While still an infant, secretly hurried into Egypt by his parents

5 Baptized by his cousin John

6 Selected the Twelve (his first disciples)

7 Rejected by his hometown (Nazareth)

8 Preached the Sermon on the Mount (possibly the greatest message ever)

9 Calmed a storm with just his words

10 Fed more than 5,000 people (on at least two occasions)

11 Right in front of three close friends, he was transfigured (for just a moment, he put on as much of his God-ness as his friends could stand without being incinerated on the spot)

12 Gave life back to Lazarus (who was dead, buried, and beginning to stink by the time Jesus arrived on the scene)

13 Blessed children

14 Was crucified, buried, and resurrected

15 Ascended into heaven

The Gospel of

Matthew

So what's Matthew's angle?

Some people's feet smell pretty bad when you're standing five or six feet away, but being down there at ground level trying to squeeze the hot, sweaty, swollen foot of some Saturday afternoon shopper into a shoe must be hellish. Pity the shoe shop worker!

Matthew's Gospel is like the shoehorn that helps fit the New Testament (the foot) into the already formed background of the Old Testament (the shoe). In Matthew, we see Jesus as the Jewish Messiah—the fulfillment of God's Old Testament promises to the Jewish people. Matthew makes the perfect link between the Old and the New Testaments.

But who was Matthew?

Matthew was the Jewish tax collector who became a disciple of Jesus.

Note the fact that only Matthew reports the strange story about Jesus, Peter, a fish, and the temple tax (read the whole thing in Matthew 17:24–27).

When did he write it?

As Matthew seems to have used Mark's Gospel as the basis of his, Matthew's must have been written later. Duh!

Since it seems to be written primarily for Jews, it was probably written in the middle of the first century when the majority of the Christians were Jewish—so sometime around A.D. 50.

Who was he writing to?

Matthew wrote especially for Jewish Christians who were being persecuted. He encourages them to use even persecution as an opportunity for evangelism.

Matthew also expected his book to be read by other people.

gift

Main themes

Old Testament prophecy

Many times I've wished I had a prophetic gift—it would improve my grade if I could predict what questions were going to be on an exam. It seems, though, that God only speaks to his prophets about important things—more important than my exams.

Event after event in Jesus' life is shown by Matthew to have been predicted by Old Testament prophets. For example—

The virgin birth—read Matthew 1:18–23

The birthplace, Bethlehem—read
Matthew 2:5–6

The entry to Jerusalem on a donkey—read
Matthew 21:4–5

In the past, people have argued that the early Christians simply invented parts of Jesus' life in order to make it conform to Old Testament prophecy. But this is not borne out by the facts.

The story of Jesus' life came first, and it was only later the disciples noticed that certain events had been predicted in the Old Testament.

Jesus' compassion

Jesus is sometimes described, especially in old versions of the Bible, as meek. You might think that's a horrible way to be described. Some people may picture a mamma's boy or a girly man. What does meekness mean?

I'll never forget a scene I saw on TV in the middle of an international rugby match. A big and exceptionally ugly, second-row forward, who shall remain nameless for that reason, was kneeling on the field with a badly injured player's head on his lap. He was holding his hand and stroking his forehead to comfort him. That's meekness—the strength of a second-row forward expressed in kindness and gentleness.

That's how we see Jesus in Matthew's Gospel. Of course, he's the Messiah, the powerful Son of God, but he is often moved by compassion for the people around him.

Jesus' manifesto

Opinions are like armpits. Everyone has a couple and most of them stink. It's not unusual for people to volunteer their opinion on how life should be lived. It is unique to find one as different, radical, and beautiful as Jesus' view.

Read all about how Jesus thought people should live and treat each other by reading the most famous sermon ever given.

MATTHEW

Interesting bits

The Sermon on the Mount (see above)
—read Matthew 5:1–7:29

The parable of the sheep and the goats
—read Matthew 25:31–46

Incredible signs accompany Jesus' death
—read Matthew 27:45–54

The Gospel of
Mark

What was Mark's angle?

Convincing your parents of the suitability of your new boyfriend can be difficult. ("But Mom, everyone's forehead is tattooed now, and body piercing is biblical—really!") But trying to convince your mom you should be involved with someone condemned to die in the electric chair would be even harder.

This is something like the problem the early Christians faced. Whatever else they told people about Jesus, eventually they had to admit Jesus was crucified. For people of that time, crucifixion was the most shameful (and difficult) death imaginable.

Mark tried to counteract the shame of Jesus' death on the cross by showing how incredible his life was.

Who was Mark?

John Mark was a man who traveled with Paul and was the cousin of Barnabas. He also acted as the Apostle Peter's interpreter.

Mark is reported to have recorded lots of short stories and anecdotes that Peter told here and there and formed them into one continuous account of Jesus' life.

When did he write it?

Mark's Gospel was probably written in the late forties of the first century A.D. when Peter was in Rome.

Who was he writing to?

Mark's careful explanations of Jewish customs and tradition imply that it was written for Gentiles, especially Romans who would have found Jesus' death on a cross offensive.

Main theme

A Gospel of action

Mark's Jesus is like Action Man—pursuing one important mission after another. Places to go, people to see, enemies to fight.

If you wanted to tell a non-Christian friend where to start reading the Bible, Mark's story—the shortest and most action-packed Gospel—might be best.

Interesting bits

Predicting the future—read Mark 13:1–37

Mystic Meg, eat your heart out. In chapter 13, Jesus predicts two future events: the destruction of the temple in Jerusalem, and the end of the world when Jesus will return in all his glory.

The Jerusalem temple was one of the biggest and most beautiful buildings in the ancient world—it was expected to last for thousands of years. In fact, Jesus was dead on. In A.D. 70 Roman soldiers invaded Jerusalem and totally destroyed the temple.

Since that happened, there's no reason to doubt Jesus' second prophecy will one day come true. He will return to gather his people to him. While it will never be possible to predict the exact time of his return, one thing is certain—it's closer now than it's ever been!

Other interesting bits

Jesus' power over the most violent demons—read Mark 5:1–20

John the Baptist's head on a plate—read Mark 6:14–29

Cost and reward of following Jesus—read Mark 10:17–31

The far-out side

There's surfing, and then there's surfing

Read Mark 4:35–41 and Mark 6:45–51.

I know I probably wouldn't have performed any better than those first disciples, but sometimes I get the impression that, because of their fear, they missed out on a lot of the fun of hanging with Jesus. Take these two water stories, for instance.

Imagine the rush of being in a small boat in a huge storm and knowing nothing bad could happen because Jesus was on board! Forget about Six Flags! You wanna know the meaning of the words *no fear*? Step out of the boat, and try surfing without a board! Okay, the ride didn't last long, but still...

MARK

dude, no board

surfing types

Did he or didn't he?

Theory 1

Some say Jesus didn't actually die. But—

Do you want to know a really good way to become a Christian? No, I'm not thinking of a Billy Graham rally. A really cool way is to start to try to prove that Jesus didn't really rise from the dead.

A number of very clever lawyers have tried to prove once and for all that it didn't happen. They wanted to help people not to be confused by all those stupid Christian stories–wasn't that sweet of them? In fact a number of people who set out to disprove the claim that Jesus rose from the grave came to believe in the literal, physical resurrection of Jesus' body from the dead. They even argue that if it were tried in a court of law, the resurrection would prove to be the only reasonable explanation of what happened.

There's no space here to examine all the evidence, but just consider these problems with the main theories of those who say Jesus didn't rise from the dead.

1. The Roman executioners who knew their job said he did.

2. The blood and watery liquid that came out of the stab wound in Jesus' side prove he died.

3. A brutal beating, six hours on a cross, and the fact that he was embalmed—wrapped up like a mummy—and placed in a tomb are all compelling.

A lovely parting gift

Theory 2

Some say the disciples stole the corpse. But—

1. The evidence is they were far too scared even to consider it.

2. Roman soldiers guarding the tomb faced execution if they let the "prisoner" escape.

3. The tomb was found in perfect order, with even the burial clothes neatly wrapped—scarcely the work of frantic grave robbers.

DID HE OR DIDN'T HE?

Smiley game-show host

Theory 3

Still others say the disciples were hallucinating or simply made the whole thing up. But—

1. Five hundred people don't hallucinate the same thing, and in 1 Corinthians 15 Paul practically begs doubters to go and ask one of the hundreds of eyewitnesses.

2. If it were all made up, why didn't the nonbelievers simply go and get the rotting, smelly corpse and throw it down in front of the overly imaginative disciples? That would have been embarrassing for them—and probably the end of their made-up resurrection stories.

3. Finally, in spite of the fact that almost all of the disciples were martyred for their belief in Jesus, not one of them ever even gave a hint that it might be a hoax. Not many con men would be so committed as to die for their scam.

Even if you don't believe the Bible is the inspired Word of God, you really have a problem trying to find a better explanation than the one put forward by Matthew, Mark, Luke, and John.

The Gospel of
Luke

What's Luke's angle?

Know-it-alls really drive me mad. Name any subject under the sun and they have facts, figures, and quotes to relate to you at great length. You're chatting happily with your best friend about the latest Tom Cruise film, and along comes Mr. or Ms. Know-It-All with information on everything from which dentist polishes Tom's sparkling white teeth to how many times a year Tom and Nicole visit the mother-in-law. Do they think we really care?

Luke is the know-it-all of the New Testament. He tells us he did lots of careful research before he wrote this orderly account to prove the truth of Christianity. Where did Jesus get his beard trimmed? Luke would have known. And, actually, I might care about that.

So Luke was a bud of Paul, huh?

It is quite likely Luke wrote his Gospel while staying in Rome with the Apostle Paul who was imprisoned there.

The Gospel of Luke is a prequel to the book of Acts and was written by the same author. For more information on him, look ahead to Acts.

When did he write it?

Luke's Gospel was written in Rome in the early 60s of the first century A.D.

Who was he writing to?

Have you ever heard of Theophilus? (I bet he loved his mom and dad for giving him that name.) That's who Luke dedicates his book to. Theophilus might have been a recent convert or a potential convert or perhaps the person who provided the money for Luke to write his books.

Luke wrote mostly for open-minded Gentiles who were genuinely interested in the historical origins of Christianity, even if they were not yet Christians themselves.

Main themes

Jesus—the man of prayer

Luke shows that Jesus was a man of prayer, praying either at or before all the important events of his life and ministry.

Jesus was praying at his baptism—read Luke 3:21

Jesus prayed all night before he chose the twelve apostles—read Luke 6:12

Jesus was praying as he was transfigured—read Luke 9:28-29

Jesus prayed before his arrest and crucifixion—read Luke 22:41

The disciples noticed the effectiveness of Jesus' prayers and decided they could use a bit of that power too, thank you very much. What Jesus taught them must have blown them away.

Abba Father. We can have no idea how radical it would have been for the Jewish disciples to be told to address their God as "my Daddy-Father." That phrase showed how totally different faith was going to be now that Jesus had come.

One for all and all for one

If you're a bit of a social activist, if you like to spend Christmas feeding the homeless or if you like working for charities, then Luke is the gospel for you.

Luke shows that Jesus was the special friend of hurting people in society. People who are rejected and hurt by others are particularly the objects of God's love given through Jesus. The sick people, the poor people, the despised people like tax collectors and prostitutes loved to be with Jesus because he treated them so well and wasn't embarrassed to be seen with them.

Women, who were considered only slightly more valuable than animals in Jesus' day (!), found a champion in Jesus. He respected them as much as any man, allowed them to listen to and be taught by him along with his closest male disciples, and, after his resurrection, he appeared to women first.

Interesting bits

For info on Jesus as a baby and a child
—read Luke 1:26–2:52

The story of the good Samaritan
—read Luke 10:25–37

The story of the lost son—read Luke 15:11–32

Increasingly incredible miracles—read Luke 8:40–56

Jesus sends out 72 missionaries—read Luke 10:1–24

A section about feasts and banquets—read Luke 14:1–24

LUKE

The Gospel of

John

What was John's angle?

When you first start going out with someone, it's all wonderful. You both act just the way you think the other person wants you to, and for a while it all seems too good to be true. Sooner or later though, you have to start getting to know the real person inside—and often that's when the trouble starts.

John wanted to take his readers to a new level of relationship with Jesus. He wanted them to know the person inside. But with Jesus, the deeper you go, the more wonderful it gets.

How did John get those details?

The best biographies—the ones that really dish the dirt—come from insiders, people close to the central character. This Gospel is full of the sort of details only an insider would remember, and the author calls himself the disciple Jesus loved. This is not pride—nowhere does he call himself by name—but it fits with what we know of the disciple John from the other Gospels.

This account is very intimate since it was written by someone who knew Jesus so well.

When did he write it?

Nobody is sure exactly when this gospel was written, but it's possible John wrote it anywhere between A.D. 60 and A.D. 90.

Main theme

Jesus, the God-man

Is it a bird? Is it a plane? No, it's the God–man.

John's Gospel helps us understand that Jesus was really God and really a man. He wasn't a man pretending to be God nor God just pretending to be a man—but both. Weird? You bet.

At the beginning of his Gospel, John makes the outrageous claim that Jesus, called the Word of God, was actually the creative force behind the formation of the universe (1:3). Then he was "clothed" in human flesh, so he could come down to earth to stay a little while with us (1:14). He did

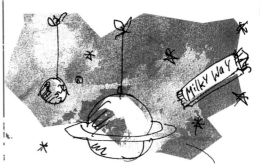

the universe

all this so he could reveal the God who was never seen before to all of us on earth (1:18).

Jesus didn't stop being God when he came to earth. John shows this especially in Jesus' I AM claims.

I AM the bread of life—read John 6:35

I AM the light of the world—read John 8:12

I AM the resurrection and the life—read John 11:25

I AM the way and the truth and the life—read John 14:6

These claims are bold. No normal man could make them unless he was (a) taking something stronger than aspirin or (b) a sandwich looking for a picnic.

But those claims didn't annoy the Jews nearly as much as when Jesus simply said, I AM (full stop). The words I AM were the ones God used to reveal himself to Moses in the Old Testament, so in these instances Jesus was making clear claims to be God. This is why in chapter 8, verses 58–59, the Jews immediately pick up stones to kill him. Stoning was the punishment for blasphemy, and of course calling yourself God was blasphemy—unless like Jesus, you really were God!

John had to balance this emphasis on Jesus as God with proof he was also really a man. He does this by showing that Jesus got tired and thirsty (4:6–7 and 19:28), he wept (11:35), and he really died before he rose again (19:30–42 and 20:10–28).

Interesting bits

The story behind the famous John 3:16 verse—read John 3:1–21

Jesus and the Samaritan woman—read John 4:1–42

Jesus protects the adulterous woman—read John 8:1–11

An evening with Jesus—read John chapters 13–17

Jesus after the resurrection—read John chapters 20–21

JOHN

TWO ROUGH PAGES

These pages have been left
blank for you to write down
things you want to remember,
things you want to forget, and
things you want to ask an
older Christian!

So over to you...

The Four Gospels

| Matthew Mark Luke John | Acts | Romans 1 Corinthian 2 Corinthians Galatia Philippians Colossia 2 Thessalonians 1 2 Timothy Titus |

The Acts of the Apostles

Paul's Letters

Other Letters

Ephesians
1 Thessalonians
Timothy
Philemon

Hebrews James
1 Peter 2 Peter
1 John 2 John 3 John
Jude

Revelation

Revelation

The Acts of the Apostles

Acts tells the story of an explosion—the dynamic beginnings of the Christian church. The fuse is lit when Jesus returns to heaven, and the flames ignite when the Holy Spirit is poured out on the disciples. There are fireworks and spectacular results as the disciples proclaim the good news about Jesus.

In a series of secondary explosions, the gospel is carried from Jerusalem to the city that was then the center of the world—Rome.

Who wrote it?

You can tell a doctor from a mile off. Even if there's no obvious visual sign—like one of those wooden tongue-depressor thingies stuck behind the ear—you can tell because he insists on calling everything by its proper medical name.

Greek scholars have noticed that the author of Acts was the sort of man who insisted on calling bad breath *halitosis*. He could only have been a doctor.

Luke, who wrote a gospel as well as recorded the Acts of the Apostles, may have been Paul's personal physician. He certainly traveled with him a lot. One of the first Gentiles to become a Christian, Luke probably lived in the city of Antioch. He knew how to look after himself because he is reputed to have lived to 84 years of age—an unusually long run for those times.

What type of writing is Acts?

Sneaking a peek into someone's electronic organizer can be fun—finding out what she's got scheduled for Saturday night, for instance. But if you get hold of her journal, then you've hit pay dirt—not just dates and appointments, but thoughts and feelings too.

The book of Acts is more like a diary than an organizer. It records past events—so it is history—but it's more than simple facts. Luke intended to show God working in the history. Luke wrote and encouraged his readers in their belief and understanding of God.

Is Acts historically true?

Fortunately for us, Luke is more Sherlock Holmes than Inspector Clouseau. He had a sharp eye for small and seemingly unimportant details and was meticulously accurate. Like any great detective he interviewed witnesses, made notes on things he saw himself, and consulted other accounts of what happened. We can trust what we read in Acts.

When and where was this book written?

Have you ever watched one of those old Saturday morning cartoons—Johnny Quest or Batman maybe? Remember the way they leave you hanging? Johnny and Hadji are about to crash and burn. Batman is about to be chopped in two by a falling ax.

Acts leaves one of its main heroes in just such a sticky predicament. Why would Luke finish his book with Paul stuck in prison and all us readers wondering whether he was going to be executed or not?

The most reasonable explanation is that this is how things stood at the time Luke wrote the book. Luke might even have written a lot of the book sitting in that prison cell in Rome with the Apostle Paul!

Why did he write it?

After returning from a vacation in Greece, you might need to write two letters: one to your Great-Aunt Maude and one to your best friend Squiggy. Just by reading the letters it would be easy to tell which was which. For instance, your aunt probably wouldn't need to know about the person you kissed/didn't quite kiss/wished you hadn't kissed.

By studying Luke's books, we can guess whom he was writing to and why. Luke probably didn't write Acts for Christians. Instead, he wrote for two groups of non-Christians.

The first group was made up of people who were genuinely interested in Christianity but not yet convinced. They needed solid proof it was not just made-up stories.

Secondly, Luke was writing for the Roman rulers. He wanted them to understand Christianity and trust that its followers were not dangerous rebels.

Outline of the book of Acts

ACTS

The Holy Spirit

Wonder Woman spun around, Superman disappeared into telephone booths to put on his red underpants, Batman went to the Batcave for his transformation—but what in the world happened to Peter?

In the gospels, Peter is loud but often incompetent and cowardly. In Acts he is transformed. He is fearless. He is able to perform powerful miracles (even his shadow could heal). He has overcome his previous foot-in-mouth disease and become a potent speaker. What happened to this man?

Luke's answer is he was filled with the Spirit. One of the main emphases of Acts is that the Holy Spirit empowers people to live the Christian life and to be witnesses for Jesus.

Good news for everyone!

Some things just don't mix. Oil and water, Friday nights and homework, basketballs and greenhouses. Add to that list Jews and the rest of the world.

The Jewish disciples suffered a severe case of selective hearing (you know what I mean—the condition that allows you to hear your mom calling, "Do you need some money?" but totally miss, "Clean up your room!") when Jesus told them to take the good news to everyone. They assumed he meant every Jew.

Around the middle of Acts, though, a totally unexpected thing happens—non-Jews start becoming Christians! In fact, within a short time they vastly outnumber the Jewish believers.

a dinner roll

an important role

The Apostle Paul

It's important to match people's abilities to the role you want them to perform. It's no use having someone clumsy and slow as a wide receiver on a football team and someone of five feet nothing as a power forward in the WNBA.

The Apostle Paul's background and abilities made him the perfect man for the job God wanted him to perform. He was a devout and academically brilliant Jew, but he was also a Roman citizen who grew up in the Gentile city of Tarsus.

To begin with, he passionately hated the Christians, but he was miraculously converted and went on to become a very important man in the New Testament. His unusual background helped him relate to and be a link between the Jews and the Gentiles. His past studies helped him to explain the Christian message better than anyone else.

Eventually he was arrested and sent to Rome where he was martyred for his faith in Jesus.

Interesting bits

Read about Paul's missionary journeys.

Journey One, 1,500 miles—Acts 13:1–14:28 —testing the water

Journey Two, 4,000 miles—Acts 15:36–18:22 —first into Europe

Journey Three, 4,000 miles—Acts 8:23–21:19 —ends in Jerusalem

In Paul's life, and particularly his missionary journeys, we see how God uses people who are willing to take outrageous risks for him.

Other interesting bits

The Holy Spirit at Pentecost—read Acts 2:1–41

Don't mess with God—read Acts 5:1–11

The conversion of Saul/Paul—read Acts 9:1–19

Tales of the high seas—read Acts 27:1–28:44

The far-out side

Read Acts 20:7–12.

Luke actually witnessed this little gem about a young man falling asleep and then falling to his death while Paul preached a monster sermon. (The man was sitting in a third-story window when he drifted off.) I think we can tell where Luke's sympathies lie because he writes that Paul was going "on and on."

Fortunately, Paul is not your average, run-of-the-mill, long-winded speaker. He may have a lot to say, but he's also got what it takes when the rubber hits the road. Rather than being struck by remorse and repentant for boring the poor guy to death, he simply goes downstairs and raises young Eutychus from the dead. Then he picks up where he left off and keeps talking…until daybreak! You have a problem with that?

As someone who's been known to nod off in a sermon from time to time, my application of this passage is that only preachers with a proven ability to raise the dead should be allowed to speak for more than 20 minutes.

ACTS

The Four Gospels

Matthew	Mark	Acts	Romans 1 Corinthia
Luke John			2 Corinthians Galati
			Philippians Colossia
			2 Thessalonians 1
			2 Timothy Titus

The Acts of the Apostles

Paul's Letters

Other Letters

Ephesians
1 Thessalonians
1mothy
1emon

Hebrews James
1 Peter 2 Peter
1 John 2 John 3 John
Jude

Revelation

Revelation

Paul the Letter Writer

Serious workaholic, insomniac, or what? Paul, the Christian-hater transformed into Christian leader, not only traveled all over the known world as a missionary, but also found time to write thirteen of the books of the New Testament.

Books or letters?

Reading other people's mail may be rude, but that's just what you're doing in a lot of the New Testament. Each of Paul's New Testament books takes the form of a letter. Some are written to whole churches or regions, and some are written to individuals.

In our Bibles, letters to whole churches come first and those written to individuals are second. Each group is arranged from the longest to the shortest.

Hey, this is deep! What does it mean?

Any snoop who's ever tried to read someone else's letters knows it's a bit like listening to one side of a telephone conversation. You can hear the answers but have to guess at the questions—you'd catch so much more if you just knew what the other person was saying.

This is why we need to know something about the people and places Paul was writing to. It's like hearing at least some of the other side of the conversation and makes reading Paul's letters much more interesting and informative.

How did he find the time?

The time to write letters might have fit into Paul's very crowded life like this:

Paul's birth	around the same time as Jesus
Paul's conversion	AD 33
First missionary journey	AD 47-48
Galatians written after return	AD 48
Council at Jerusalem	AD 49
Second missionary journey	AD 49-52
1 and 2 Thessalonians written	AD 52
Third missionary journey	AD 52-56
1 and 2 Corinthians written	AD 55
Romans written	AD 56
Arrest in Jerusalem	AD 56
Journey to Rome	AD 60-61
In Rome under guard	AD 61
Philemon, Colossians, Ephesians, and Philippians written	AD 61
Released and free to travel	AD 62-66
1 Timothy and Titus written	AD 62-65

Paul arrested and imprisoned in Rome	AD 66–67
2 Timothy written	AD 67
Paul executed	AD 67

Why did he write his letters?

There's a book that begins with the words: "Life is difficult." No one disagrees. And life may never be more difficult than in the wild mental, emotional, and physical growth spurts of adolescence.

The churches Paul started were going through adolescence. And, like human teenagers, the growing up involved testing some boundaries and getting into some trouble.

The churches looked to Paul, their founder, as a kind of father figure, and they expected his help. Since he couldn't be everywhere at once, he often wrote letters.

But are they really letters?

Paul would have gotten top marks from his English teacher (or, more accurately, his Greek teacher) for letter composition. All his letters are written in the correct style and form of the day.

Paul probably dictated them to a professional secretary or scribe, who probably found it hard to keep up with the rushing Paul. As this person wrote with aching hands and fingers, I suspect he would have killed for a laptop!

Paul often wrote the last few lines of his letters himself to act as a signature, maybe as a guarantee that the letter wasn't forged in his name.

The letter to the

Romans

The city of Rome

Geography—Rome was the center of the universe—or of the massive Roman Empire at least. In the ancient world it was said that all roads led to Rome.

Population—Rome was also the largest city in the world, with between 1 and 4 million people. The capital attracted men and women from every country, and wealthy kings and lords mixed on every street with beggars and slaves.

Politics—There was a new emperor, Nero, and his guards and soldiers were everywhere, carrying out his wishes not just in the city but throughout the known world.

The church in Rome

One ancient historian must have failed his spelling tests—he records that the Emperor Claudius threw all the Jews out of Rome because they were rioting about someone named *Chrestus*. This may be a misspelled Latin form of *Christ*, in which case the historian is telling us the church in Rome began before the end of Claudius' reign.

Like the people of many capital cities, it seems the Roman Christians were proud. This caused friction since both Jews and Gentiles wanted to be in charge.

Why did Paul write this letter?

Now, let me think…I could invite myself around to stay with some wealthy Roman Christians for a few weeks. Then I could take up a collection and that would pay for a nice vacation on the Costa del Sol in sunny Spain. Bingo—it's a plan!

I wouldn't dare imply that was how the great Apostle Paul thought, but that was roughly his purpose in writing the letter to the Romans. He wanted to establish contact and prepare the Romans for his coming to stay. And one of his hopes was that the wealthy people of the capital city would be able to provide him with money to take another, even more far-reaching, missionary journey to Spain.

The other side of the conversation

By studying Paul's letter to the Romans, we can tell these are the questions they would have been asking him—

1. How should Christians treat government authorities?

2. How can something as invisible as faith save us?

3. If we're completely forgiven, do we still have to obey rules?

4. Are Jewish Christians better off than Gentiles with God?

As you read through Romans, see if you can recognize where Paul is answering these questions.

Main theme

Great save!

The book of Romans has been compared to dynamite, and at the risk of psyching you out, I'd say to you: don't read it unless you're ready to have your mind blown and your life changed. Great church leaders like Martin Luther and John Wesley were deeply affected by the book of Romans. So what got to them?

The teaching that most affected them was that Christians are saved not by any action they take, but because of what Jesus has already done. According to Paul, we are saved by faith alone. That may not seem too radical to you, but in other stages of the church's history, it was explosive.

Interesting bits

Downward spiral of humanity without God—read Romans 1:18–32

Nothing can separate us from God's love—read Romans 8:28–39

Practical advice for living—read Romans 12:1–14:40

ROMANS

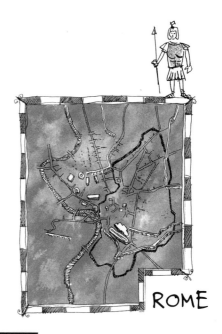

ROME

The letters to the
Corinthians

The city of Corinth

Geography—Corinth was situated on a very narrow strip of land between the two parts of Greece. Small boats were actually dragged from one side to the other on rollers.

Population—It was a large and very busy city with around 700,000 people. There was a particularly high number of slaves in Corinth.

Politics—At the time of Paul's letters, Corinth was an important Roman colony and the capital of the Roman province of Achaia.

Sports—Corinth held famous games, second only to the Olympics in popularity.

Religion—Corinth was a pagan city, although Jews also lived there. The most important deity was Aphrodite, goddess of love and beauty.

Morality—If Corinth were a film, it would be rated NC-17. One writer said Corinth was "a seaman's paradise, a drunkard's heaven, and a virtuous woman's hell."

The church

Paul spent one and a half years in Corinth (Acts 18), and started the church, but it always seemed to have its problems.

There were both Jews and Greeks among the believers. Perhaps unsurprisingly in such an immoral city, the new believers seemed to struggle with Christian conduct. Sexual sins seem to have been a particular problem for the Corinthians, so there is much we can learn from these letters to help us in our sex-crazed society.

Paul's view of marriage

1 Corinthians

Why did Paul write this letter?

Have you ever had a friend who was so competitive you couldn't put your socks on or pick your nose without it becoming a competition? "Mine's bigger and greener than yours!" Some people are competitive to the point of insanity.

The Corinthians were like that, and they carried the competitive attitudes of their famous sporting games into church with them. Paul heard of rivalries among leaders in the church and also received a letter asking specific questions. He was worried, so he wrote 1 Corinthians to them.

The other side of the conversation

From Paul's response, we can guess at some of the questions the letter from Corinth asked him. Here are some of the key ones—

1. We disagree about which Christian leader to follow. What should we do?

2. Is marriage a good or a bad thing?

3. How can we use spiritual gifts without becoming competitive?

Look for Paul's answers to these questions when you read 1 Corinthians.

Main theme

Large companies sometimes employ professional problem solvers called troubleshooters. It's okay. They're not hit men or anything. Their job is to use their experience to make the company work better in areas where there are major holdups (these are not robberies but merely rough spots in the business).

The main theme of 1 Corinthians is the various troubles in the church. Practically everything Paul says in this letter is correcting the way things were done or the way people thought in the Corinthian church. Paul is working as a troubleshooter.

Interesting bits

Paul's view of marriage—read 1 Corinthians 7:1–40

The famous love chapter—read 1 Corinthians 13:1–13

The resurrection equals victory over death—read 1 Corinthians 15:1–58

2 Corinthians

Why did Paul write a second letter?

Laurel and Hardy, although funny, can be excruciatingly frustrating to watch. You know the situation is going to get worse and worse before it gets better.

Paul must have had that kind of frustrated feeling about Corinth. No matter what he did, things got worse and worse. Having written 1 Corinthians to them and made a flying visit from where he was living in Ephesus, Paul found they were still as much a mess as ever. It seems in the end he had to be very hard on them to straighten them out.

He wrote another letter, which unfortunately (or perhaps fortunately for the pride of the Corinthians) has been lost. In it he told them in no uncertain terms to sort out their lives. Finally they came round, and 2 Corinthians was written after all of that to assure them he still loved and cared for them.

this year's hat

The other side of the conversation

Some of the ground Paul covered answered questions the Corinthians might have had like—

1. How can we judge who are true ministers of God, if not by their talents and status?

2. How can we learn to view people as Jesus does and not just according to their social standing?

3. How can God use us when we're weak?

Watch for answers to these questions as you read through 2 Corinthians.

Main theme

Daydream break. You're leaning on a bright red Porsche convertible on the beach front in Malibu. You're wearing sunglasses so expensive they make Oakleys look like the plastic toy in a cereal box. Your clothes are straight out of *Vogue* or *GQ*, and every one of the beautiful people wandering along the beach stops to stare at you. Okay, you can wake up now.

It's image that counts, right? That's what a lot of people think. If I can just wear the right clothes and be seen with the right people, life will be perfect.

That's what the Corinthians believed. Nothing was as important as what people thought of them. They had to look great, dress right, live in the right area of the city, and have a reputation for being talented at what they did. Paul still needed to straighten them out some more.

Strange as it may seem, one of the main themes of 2 Corinthians is boasting. The Corinthians were used to boasting about their wealth or their intelligence or their important positions.

Paul was very clear in telling them these weren't the sort of things Christians should be proud of. Paul said Christians may only boast about their weaknesses—because this is what Christ is able to work through. That teaching must have gone straight to the heart of the proud Corinthians.

Interesting bits

Christians are like Christ's ambassadors— read 2 Corinthians 5:16–21

Read about all that Paul had suffered—read 2 Corinthians 11:16–33

CORINTH

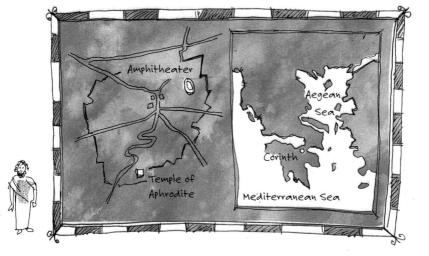

Amphitheater

Temple of Aphrodite

Aegean Sea

Corinth

Mediterranean Sea

The letter to the Galatians

Geography

This letter was written to four cities in the Roman province of Galatia that Paul visited on his first missionary journey.

Why did Paul write this letter to churches in Galatia?

A friend of mine once belonged to a very elite group of swimmers. They decided that to join their group you not only had to be a fast enough swimmer, but you also had to agree to follow their rules. This included shaving all the hair off your head and body before big races. It was supposed to make you feel part of the group and also to cut down on drag as you swam through the water. Yeah, right! For some would-be members that was asking too much and they never joined the group.

In Galatia, the Jewish Christians were forcing the Gentile Christians to obey their Jewish rules. They said following Jesus was not enough. If you wanted to be a real Christian, you had to become a Jew.

One of their main demands was that the male converts be circumcised (an eye-watering and excruciatingly painful experience for an adult man). Paul was angry about what the Jewish Christians were saying, and he wrote to tell them circumcision had nothing to do with following Jesus and they'd better keep their blades in the sheaths.

The other side of the conversation

False teachers in the Galatian area argued Christianity was a part of the Jewish religion and therefore converts must become Jews. The questions that seemed to have reached Paul were—

1. Must Gentile converts be circumcised and live out the Jewish way of life?

2. If they refuse, are they second-class Christians?

As you read Galatians, look for the points at which Paul answers these questions.

Main theme

So embarrassing! Have you ever received a really expensive Christmas present from a friend you never even thought of buying for? You feel so bad that often, even though you've already been given the gift, you try to earn it. You start being incredibly nice to your friend, phoning her every night, making sure you invite her every time you go out, trying to set her up with your boyfriend… okay, maybe not that nice.

Paul had to explain to the Galatian Christians that there was nothing they could do to earn God's love and salvation. God gave them as free gifts, and no effort of theirs could accomplish any more.

He said it was okay if Jewish Christians wanted to go on following the Jewish laws, but it didn't make them any better than people who didn't.

Interesting bits

Paul argues with Peter about the rules—read Galatians 2:11–21

We are not God's slaves but his children—read Galatians 4:1–7

The far-out side

Read Galatians 5:12.

Harsh words here from an apostle of God. He is really angry about the false teachers trying to put Gentiles under the Jewish laws. He tells them he wishes they wouldn't just circumcise themselves; he'd like them to go the whole way and castrate themselves. Then the Galatian church could have had a nice choir of men with high voices!

That's gotta hurt

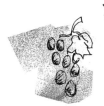

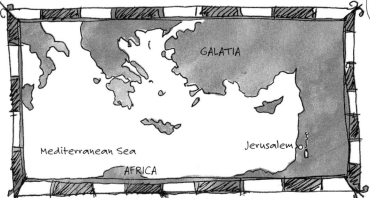

ROMAN PROVINCE OF GALATIA

GALATIA

Mediterranean Sea

AFRICA

Jerusalem

GALATIANS

The letter to the
Ephesians

Ephesus the city

Geography—Ephesus was located at the mouth of the Cayster River. It was a busy seaport because it was located at the western end of the great overland trade route to the East.

Politics—Although it wasn't the capital, Ephesus was considered the first city because it was so busy and wealthy—a bit like New York City.

Religion—Ephesus was another pagan city and the home to another goddess—the goddess Diana (called Artemis by the Greeks). The temple built for the goddess in Ephesus was one of the seven wonders of the ancient world. Her statue in the temple was supposed to have fallen from heaven.

Entertainment—With the largest Roman theater in Asia Minor, as well as many other attractions, Ephesus was an entertainment capital.

The church

Paul spent a number of years in Ephesus on his second and third missionary journeys. As usual, the people of the city had a sort of love-hate relationship with him—the Christians loved him, and everybody else hated him.

The people he particularly ticked off in Ephesus were the craftsmen who made little souvenirs of the statue of Diana for all the tourists. Their gripe was that Paul let the secret out of the bag by telling everybody the Greek gods, like Diana, were not gods at all.

Nobody wanted to buy pretty little statues any more, and the craftsmen were feeling the pinch. When they rioted, Paul wanted to preach to them, but somebody explained that sometimes discretion is the better part of valor and helped him to escape. The church contained both Gentile and Jewish Christians, and in later centuries it grew to become the largest and most important church in that region.

Why did Paul write this letter?

Unlike Paul's other letters, there really is no other side to the conversation. The letter is not written in response to any major problems or questions on the part of the Ephesian church. It has a positive feel and was written by Paul during his imprisonment in Rome—when presumably he had plenty of time on his hands.

Main theme

I'd never say it to their faces, but it's easy to assume body-builders are not just thick in the biceps if you know what I mean; not the brightest bulbs on a tree if you get my drift; not playing with a full deck if you follow me. Does anybody remember where I was going with this? Ah, yes. I automatically assume bodybuilders aren't particularly clever. This is certainly not fair, but I tend to think if they're that focused on their bodies, spending hours every day in the gym, they may be neglecting their heads.

Paul often uses the analogy that Christ is the head and the church is his body. In that case, the book of Ephesians is bodybuilder paradise

Paul with Thyme on his hands

In Ephesians, Paul concentrates on how the body of Christ, the church, can be built up into Mr. Universe-type proportions. For Paul, unity is like the latest bulk-building, high-protein drink the Ephesians need if they are to grow big and strong. He talks about unity in deeply spiritual ways, but also very practically.

Interesting bits

Paul's prayer for the Ephesians—read Ephesians 3:14–21

Children and parents—read Ephesians 6:1–4

Fight the spiritual battle—read Ephesians 6:10–20

EPHESIANS

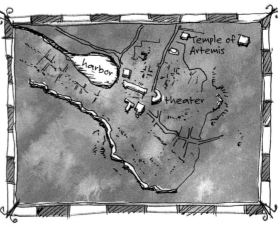

EPHESUS

Temple of Artemis

harbor

theater

The letter to the
Philippians

The city Philippi

Geography—Philippi was in Macedonia and located on a fertile plain about 10 miles inland from the Aegean Sea.

Politics—The city was named after Alexander the Great's father, Philip. Philippi was a Roman colony and was an important trading station since it was built on a busy road called the Ignatian Way.

Fame—Philippi was famous for its gold deposit and for its medical school where some people believe Luke the New Testament writer studied.

The church

Every teacher has her favorite pupil. If you forget your homework it's double detention for sure, but if the teacher's pet doesn't bring it, then the teacher is all concerned: "Is everything okay? Is there anything I can do?"

If Paul had a favorite church, it would appear to have been the Philippians. He started the church on his second missionary journey, and it was in Philippi that Paul and Silas were miraculously released from prison by an earthquake. So Paul undoubtedly had some fond memories of Philippians.

Since there was no Jewish synagogue in Philippi, it's likely the Christians were all Gentiles.

Why did Paul write the letter?

Like all good, well-mannered children, Paul was taught to write thank-you notes for gifts he received. His granny got one, so did Auntie Mildred, and also the Philippian church. It's apparently not the first time they supported him, although I'm sure that had nothing to do with their status as teacher's pet.

Their latest gift gets this thank-you letter, with a few added morsels of theology.

The other side of the conversation

Epaphroditus, who carried the gift to Paul, obviously had information on how the church was going in Philippi. He could have asked Paul any questions the Christians had. Their concerns seem to have been—

1. How are you doing, Paul? Those of us in Philippi are worried about your suffering. (Doesn't that sound just like a teacher's pet!)

2. What sort of conduct does Christ's humility require of his followers?

3. Are you certain we don't need to become Jews?

As you read Philippians, look for Paul's answers to these questions.

Main theme

The school outing to the theme park has been canceled, and an exam is scheduled in its place. What you really need is a period of feeling sorry for yourself, a day of mood swings so everyone knows how unlucky you are. But there's always some cheery, ever-pleasant person who wants to tell you to count your blessings and look on the bright side—after all, every cloud has a silver lining—but all you want to do is strangle him.

The main theme of Philippians is joy. Although Paul is in prison and could soon be executed, he is still joyful and unconcerned—to live is Christ, to die is gain (1:21). He wants the Philippians to experience the same joy he has.

Interesting bits

A hymn of the early church about Jesus— read Philippians 2:5–11

Paul's early successes are rubbish compared to knowing Jesus—read Philippians 3:4–11

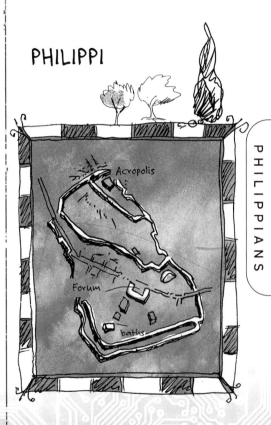

PHILIPPI

PHILIPPIANS

Acropolis

Forum

baths

The letter to the

Colossians

The city of Colosse

Geography—The city lies in the valley of the Lycus River, in a mountainous region about 100 miles east of Ephesus.

History—Colosse may have started its life as a military fort because it was strategically placed in a defendable valley on an important trade route.

Fame—"Hey, look at those sheep!" Colosse was famous for its sheep, whose purple wool was sold for lots and lots of money.

The church

"If Dad's out of his league, perhaps Granddad can help" seems to be the thought of the Colossians.

Paul hadn't started or even visited the church in Colosse. It seems a man named Epaphras, who had been converted by Paul in Ephesus and then had gone back to his hometown of Colosse, had founded it. The problems in Colosse were obviously too big for Epaphras to handle, so he traveled all the way to Rome to ask the advice of Paul, his father in the faith and a sort of granddaddy to the church.

Why did Paul write to the Colossians?

It seems a particular false teaching had entered the church in Colosse. The weird ideas of what might have been a sort of Christian secret society included—
• believing that secret information saves you
• not thinking Christ was very important
• worshiping angels as messengers between man and God
• following some of the Jewish laws and customs

The other side of the conversation

For Epaphras to travel all the way to Rome from Colosse shows he was pretty desperate—there being no nonstop flights in those days. When he got to Paul, he would undoubtedly have made the most of the opportunity to pick his brains.

From the letter Paul sent back to Colosse, it seems these were the questions Epaphras was asking—

1. How can I tell which religious leader to listen to?

2. How should a real Christian live?

3. Is there secret knowledge that only some Christians have?

As you read, see how Paul responded to these questions.

Main theme

If the French Revolution taught us nothing else, it taught us (thanks to the invention of the guillotine) that bodies no longer connected to their heads die. (Some reports say it took a few seconds—eyes in unattached heads looking around and even mouths speaking.)

If Ephesians was the bodybuilders' letter, then Colossians is the letter about the importance of the head. Paul focuses his attention on Christ as the head of the church because the Colossians had begun to doubt his importance. Paul stresses that Christ is always the most important because he maintains the whole universe, saves humanity, and oversees the church.

Interesting bits

Christ, master of the universe—read Colossians 1:15–20

How Christians should live—read Colossians 3:1–17

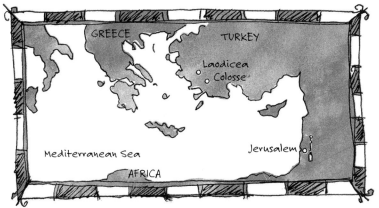

COLOSSE

The letters to the
Thessalonians

The city Thessalonica

Geography—Thessalonica is a natural harbor, and in Paul's time it was the capital city of the Roman province of Macedonia.

Population—Thessalonica was an important trading city, and it had many nonnative inhabitants, including Jews.

The church

Paul spent about one month in Thessalonica on his second missionary journey. He was forced to leave because the unbelieving Jews were rioting and trying to kill him. He left some of his helpers behind to continue the work, and a church, made up mostly of Gentiles, was started.

I Thessalonians

Why did Paul write the first letter to the Thessalonians?

Have you ever seen news reports about the street children of South America? Five- and six-year-olds living alone on the streets, stealing and fighting to stay alive. Harsh conditions force children to grow up fast.

Paul wrote this first letter only a few weeks after he left the Thessalonians, so they were baby Christians. But in an environment of violent persecution, they had to grow up fast. Paul wrote to encourage them in their new faith and to tell them about the great Christian hope of Jesus' second coming and heaven.

The other side of the conversation

Quite understandably, the Thessalonian Christians thought they might have made a big mistake. What kind of religion is it that can get you killed so easily? They wanted to know—

1. What happens to Christians who die?

2. Is all this trouble because God is angry?

3. Does all this persecution have any benefits?

See how Paul answers these questions as you read
1 Thessalonians.

THESSALONICA

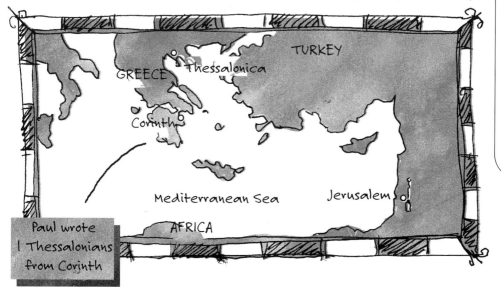

TURKEY

GREECE Thessalonica

Corinth

Mediterranean Sea   Jerusalem

AFRICA

Paul wrote
1 Thessalonians
from Corinth

Main theme

The dentist will sometimes promise a little child a balloon as soon as he's finished poking around in her mouth. That hope might give her the strength to endure the discomfort of having 10 fingers and five tools stuck in her mouth.

In the same way, hope is the main theme of Paul's first letter to the Thessalonians. He knows they are having a hard time, and he wants to encourage them. Particularly, he encourages them by telling them that one day Jesus will come back and all Christians will go to heaven to be with him.

Interesting bits

Good examples—read 1 Thessalonians 1:4–10

Be encouraged: Jesus will return—read 1 Thessalonians 4:13–5:11

2 Thessalonians

Why did Paul write a second letter?

Have you ever been under so much pressure you actually thought you were going to lose it? You start to have visions of accidentally introducing yourself as Napoleon or forgetting to dress before you leave for school in the morning.

Well, the young Thessalonian Christians were under so much pressure they became fanatics. They wanted Jesus to come back and save them from persecution so much they made themselves believe they could practically hear him coming.

The other side of the conversation

If the Thessalonians were to calm down, they needed answers to questions like these—

1. Why doesn't God punish evil people who hurt Christians?

2. Is it true we're in the final evil days of the Antichrist?

As the millenium turned, many Christians turned up the heat predicting Jesus' return. As you read 2 Thessalonians, see what Paul has to say about that.

Main theme

Have you ever asked yourself, "Is it worth it?" Perhaps as you sat down to yet another marathon night of homework or as you pumped out your 200th pushup. "Can passing my exams or making the team possibly be worth this?"

In 2 Thessalonians Paul says, "Don't give up—stand firm!" Like an athletic coach, he encouraged them to keep going to the end!

Interesting bits

Encouragement to keep going—read 2 Thessalonians 2:13–17

Christians should not be lazy—read 2 Thessalonians 3:6–15

The letters to
Timothy

I Timothy

Who was Timothy?

Little brothers and sisters can have you tearing your hair out as they tag along and copy you. But it's also quite nice to know that however much they might try to hide it, there's a bit of hero worship going on—with you as the hero!

Timothy was something of a little brother to Paul, or a son in the faith as Paul puts it. He became a Christian under Paul's ministry and then insisted on tagging along with him on his second and third missionary journeys. Soon Paul trusted Timothy enough to appoint him the leader of the growing church in Ephesus.

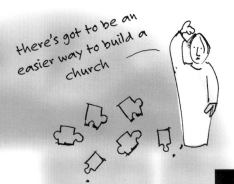

there's got to be an easier way to build a church

Why did Paul write him a letter?

There are two ways of making a model. You can simply spread the parts all over the floor, pick up the biggest and most interesting bits, and start gluing. That was always my method, which possibly explains why everything I made came out looking the same—a mixture between a double-decker bus and a deformed elephant. Or you can read the instructions and proceed in a step-by-step manner. As a young man with a very big job on his hands, Timothy needed all the help he could get. His big brother didn't let him down. Paul wrote 1 Timothy to him, giving him some step-by-step advice on how to get the church up and running.

Main theme

Just wanting something isn't enough, or I'd have played baseball for the New York Yankees long ago. You have to have the necessary qualities.

Paul's instructions to Timothy showed him what it was that made a good Christian leader. It's not wrong, said Paul, to want to be a leader, but in addition to the desire, you must have other qualifications. Leaders must be respected inside and outside the church, they mustn't be too young in their faith, and they must be self-controlled.

Qualifications for Christian leaders—read
1 Timothy 3:1–13

Being satisfied is being truly wealthy—read
1 Timothy 6:6–10

The challenge to all Christian youth—read
1 Timothy 6:11–21

2 Timothy

Why did Paul write another letter to Tim?

I can remember a moment of stunned silence in an international athletic competition. It was the men's 4x100m, and the home team was doing well. The third runner took off, and it looked as if we had a real shot. Then the stunned silence...the crowd realized the baton wasn't in the runner's hand. It had been dropped, and the race was over.

2 Timothy was the last letter Paul wrote, and when he wrote it, he knew his death was near. As an old leader, he knew the baton must be handed over to someone younger, and it couldn't be dropped. So he wrote to encourage Timothy to keep going no matter how hard things were and to continue the work Paul had started.

Main theme

If you've ever played with a terrier, you'll know why that breed has a reputation for never giving up. Once the dog's got that toy in its mouth, you're never going to get it back again.

Paul wrote to Timothy to encourage him to be persistent. He used the examples of soldier, farmer, and athlete to persuade Timothy to keep going no matter what the cost.

Paul remembers Timothy's background—read 2 Timothy 1:3–7

Timothy: soldier, athlete, and farmer—read 2 Timothy 2:1–7

1 TIMOTHY / 2 TIMOTHY

The letter to

Titus

Cleaning up

Have you ever had the feeling that all the worst jobs have some kind of homing device directing them straight at you? It's classroom cleanup time at the end of term. Fred's taking textbooks back to the storeroom. Others are auctioning off the contents of the lost-and-found closet to the highest bidder. And you? You're pulling used, and still sticky, bits of chewing gum off the underside of desks—with your teeth!

Titus must have had a similar feeling. His friend Timothy is in Ephesus—beautiful city, wonderful people, pleasure capital of the world. And Titus? He's assigned to a little rock in the middle of the sea called Crete.

What's Crete famous for? It's famous for inhabitants who are lazy, compulsive liars, and talented at nothing but eating. Just the place to be assigned to as a church leader. Paul must have known he'd given Titus the short end of the stick because he quickly wrote to him with some tips on how to get by.

Main theme

Do you know any hypocrites? (Be careful as you answer that question—you never know if someone else's finger might be pointing back at you.) Probably we all know a hypocrite or two.

Lots of people have said they think Jesus was great, and they'd willingly be his followers if it weren't for the fact that all the Christians they know are hypocrites. This is something we as Christians need to consider carefully.

Paul knew the way the Cretins lived, and he told Titus to make sure any who became Christians changed their lifestyle as well as their beliefs. He didn't want Titus to have any hypocrites in his church.

Interesting bits

Advice for different groups of people—read Titus 2:1–10

Christians should live good lives—read Titus 3:1–10

The letter to

Philemon

Cut this slave some slack

There's an old joke that goes like this: What's worse than biting into an apple and finding a worm? Biting into an apple and finding half a worm!

Things are not always as good as they appear on the surface. The Roman Empire looked like a civilized society on the surface, but beneath the skin of happy, wealthy people was a core of brutality and many, many poor and powerless men and women. Some of the most cruelly mistreated were the slaves.

This one-chapter letter to Philemon concerns a slave named Onesimus who ran away from his master. This meant if he was ever caught, he could immediately be executed.

Hiding out in Rome, a big, busy city where questions were least likely to be asked, Onesimus ran into Paul and was converted. Through coincidence, or perhaps "God-incidence," Paul knew the slave's master, Philemon, who was also a believer. So Paul wrote to him.

Main theme

The main theme of Philemon is the relationship between Christians. By law Philemon, as Onesimus' master, had the right to kill him for what he did. But Paul argues that Philemon shouldn't because Onesimus is now his brother in Christ. Paul demonstrates true Christian love by offering to pay anything Onesimus owes Philemon.

Paul asks Philemon to take Onesimus back and not punish him. He even implies Philemon might like to set him free. This would be very radical behavior for a Roman slave owner. For Onesimus' sake we can only hope Philemon took Paul's advice.

Interesting bits

How Christians should treat one another— read verses 8–20

TITUS / PHILEMON

TWO MORE ROUGH PAGES

Some more blank pages for your doodles, news, thoughts, and questions. If you really wanted more information, who would you go to with your questions?

The Four Gospels

| Matthew Mark Luke John | Acts | Romans 1 Corinthia 2 Corinthians Galatia Philippians Colossia 2 Thessalonians 1 2 Timothy Titus |

The Acts of the Apostles

Paul's Letters

Other Letters

Ephesians
1 Thessalonians
mothy
ilemon

Hebrews James
1 Peter 2 Peter
1 John 2 John 3 John
Jude

Revelation

Revelation

page 89

The letter to the
Hebrews

When artists paint, they choose one central point as their focus. Everything else in the picture guides the viewer's eye toward that point.

In Hebrews, Jesus is seen as the focus that all history points to.

Who wrote Hebrews?

Trying to decide who wrote Hebrews is like trying to pick one criminal from a lineup of the usual suspects. In this case, those under suspicion include Paul, Barnabas, Luke, Apollos, Silas, or even Priscilla (who, as a woman, might have chosen not to put her name on the letter because of the prejudice against her sex. But wouldn't she have called it "Shebrews"?).

We will never know for certain who wrote Hebrews until he or she 'fesses up in heaven.

Who was it written to?

Like Paul's letters, the title "Hebrews" reflects the people it was written to—that is, Jewish (Hebrew) Christians. It was most likely written to the Hebrew Christians in Rome sometime in the 60s of the first century A.D.

Why was it written?

Have you ever noticed it takes a conscious effort to tidy a bedroom, but no effort at all to make one messy—it just happens. Next time your mother complains, you can explain to her that it's due to the second law of thermodynamics, which states that if left without outside influence, systems (bedrooms) always degenerate (get messy). Check with your physics teacher—it's a real physical law.

Churches, like bedrooms, tend to go downhill. It seems the church in Rome had been persecuted from the outside, and on the inside things were becoming messy. They had split into rival groups that didn't meet together anymore.

Hebrews might have been written to a group of Jewish Christians who had gone their own way and, because of persecution, were now wondering: "Wouldn't it be better if we just went back to being normal Jews?"

"Absolutely no way, José," is what the writer to the Hebrews told them!

Main themes

A better way

"This is no upgrade—we're talking a whole new model here."

Most computers today can be upgraded. Simply take out the old component and put in a new one. If you upgraded your computer with the latest state-of-the-art, super-duper processor, but then found it was more trouble than it was worth—you'd take it back, demand a refund, and get your good old chip back, wouldn't you?

It seems this was how the Hebrews felt. They'd tried this newfangled Christianity, and frankly they were pretty unimpressed. They hadn't planned on having to be polite to those Gentile types for one thing, and persecution was definitely not what they signed up for.

The writer to the Hebrews had to straighten them out. Jesus wasn't just an alternative to the old way of doing things. He was superior in every way and to every person the Jews respected in the Old Testament.

This wasn't just an upgrade—it was a whole new way of doing things. Now that God had put the new system on the market, he wasn't supporting the old one. It was *do it the new and better way, or don't do it at all*.

Jesus as priest and sacrifice

"Oh, that's such a sweet little lamb. What are you going to do with it? No, you're joking! You're not going to... Does anyone else smell mint sauce?"

In the Old Testament, priests offered animal sacrifices to cover people's sins—but of course this didn't really do away with sin; it was simply a sign of what would one day happen. The real sacrifice for sin was when Jesus died on the cross. The book of Hebrews explains how this worked.

Interesting bits

Jesus, the better great high priest—read Hebrews 4:14–16

A better agreement between God and man—read Hebrews 8:1–13

Great men and women of faith—read Hebrews 11:1–40

Christians should follow Jesus' example—read Hebrews 12:1–13:17

The letter from

James

"Just do it!" It might sell athletic shoes now (and fine shoes they are), but James could well win the court battle for the right to the expression since he coined it 2,000 years ago. His advice was, "If you want to be a real Christian, don't talk about it...just do it!"

Who wrote it?

Sibling rivalry is what polite sociologists call it. World War 3 might be more appropriate to describe what goes on in some families. Brothers and sisters might love one another, but that doesn't stop them from fighting. If you've got a juicy zit on your forehead, then no one's going to enjoy telling you more than your big brother. If a girl phoned to say that actually she's changed her mind and she'd rather contract bubonic plague than go to the movies with you, then you can bet your little sister is going to enjoy giving you the message.

One of the most amazing evidences for the truth of Jesus' claims is that his family came to believe he really was God. He must have been quite an incredible brother!

There are several people named James mentioned in the New Testament, but only one is a standout contender for author of this book—that is, James the half brother of Jesus. He was the son of Mary and Joseph, but only half brother to Jesus because Jesus was conceived in the womb of Mary by the power of the Holy Spirit.

After Jesus' death and resurrection, James joined the church and became one of it's leaders in Jerusalem.

What became of James?

The historian Eusebius tells us James prayed so much he had knees as tough as a camel's. In an attempt to make him give up his faith, the Jewish leaders dragged him to the top of the temple in Jerusalem. When he got there, instead of admitting he was wrong, he started to preach about Jesus. They responded by throwing him off. When that didn't kill him, they stoned him.

Since he was martyred in A.D. 62, we know the book of James must have been written before then.

Who was it written to?

The first verse of James states that the book is written to Jewish believers who "are scattered among the nations." They probably were scattered because of the persecution in Jerusalem.

James obviously felt they needed some encouragement, not only to make it through the persecution, but also to live lives that reflected their Christian faith.

Main theme

Doctors and nurses have some rather unpleasant methods of deciding how deeply unconscious a patient is. They might stick pins into her or, if they're feeling compassionate, they might just give her earlobe a good hard pinch.

James had his own test to see if your faith is really alive. He said what you believe will come out in how you act. To paraphrase: if you don't act like a Christian, you're not a Christian. Ouch!

The areas he was particularly interested in included resisting temptation, treating people equally whether they are rich or poor, controlling what you say, and having the right attitude about money. All these issues are very much alive today.

Interesting bits

Don't just listen; act—read James 1:19–27

Treat everyone equally, whether rich or poor—read James 2:1–13

The power of words—read James 3:1–12

The power of prayer—read James 5:13–18

JAMES

The letters from

Peter

Who wrote these letters?

If the central characters of the New Testament were to be given Olympic medals, the author of these letters, Peter, might well get silver (Jesus gets gold, of course). Peter was one of Jesus' first disciples and the leader Jesus said he would build his church on.

These letters were probably written from Rome, which Peter refers to in the letters as Babylon—perhaps it was a code to keep his whereabouts secret—sometime around A.D. 65.

What happened to Peter?

Tradition says Peter was martyred in Rome. The Romans intended to crucify Peter, but he was so humble he didn't believe he was worthy to die in the same way as his Lord Jesus. So, at his request, they crucified him upside down.

Who did he write his letters to?

When they try, the post office actually is very good at deciphering bad or incomplete addresses on letters, but they would have had trouble with Peter's letters. They simply say—To Christians spread all over the place. Fortunately, he would

have sent them with a special messenger and not a mailman (or a femailman for that matter).

I Peter

Why did he write this letter?

What would you be willing to give up for the man or woman you love? Talk is easy: "I'd give up everything for you; I'd even die for you." In real life it's more like: "I might miss 'Friends' for you. Just this once, though, and only if you promise to tape it for me."

It wasn't talk for the early Christians, though. Right from the beginning they knew if they got involved with this Jesus character, they would have to be willing to give up everything—maybe even their lives. Peter wrote to help people struggling with the cost of following Jesus.

Main theme

Being second is always easier

Did you ever watch technical climbers work their way up a sheer rock face? It's tough going—searching for handholds and friction points and cracks wide enough for a fist jam. It's especially hazardous for the lead climber because she has no one above her to help if she falls. After all, the lead climber carries the front of the rope. She's looking for a good spot to set up protection for the ones who follow.

Peter reminded the persecuted Christians that they were following their Lord Jesus who suffered before them. His death on the cross was the ultimate example of unjust suffering, but it made it possible for all humanity to be brought back into relationship with God. So Peter reminds his readers that Jesus understands and he's there every minute.

Interesting bits

We are God's chosen people—read 1 Peter 2:4–10

The beauty of a holy woman—read 1 Peter 3:1–6

Special advice for young men—read 1 Peter 5:5–11

2 Peter

Why did he write another letter?

If you've ever had an enemy, you'll know there are two ways he can attack you: the obvious bash-your-face-in way, and the subtle spread-vicious-lies-through-the-whole-school way.

The early church, like the church today, had a very real enemy—Satan. In his first letter, Peter dealt with the enemy's obvious method—persecution. In 2 Peter, he deals with the enemy's sly, subtle attack on the church—false teaching.

Main theme

By the age of 16 you really ought to be able to make your own decisions about what clothes you wear. "But Mom, I really don't like wearing black socks and brown sandals any more. I feel like a tourist. What's more, my girlfriend hates them!" Part of growing up is getting to make your own choices.

Peter lays the facts in front of the Christians as plainly as he can and then allows them to make their choices. They must decide between what he is teaching and what the new false teachers are saying.

Interesting bits

Peter talks about Jesus based on what Peter actually saw and heard—read 2 Peter 1:16–18

Peter's opinion of the false teachers—read 2 Peter 2:17–22

Paul's letters are known as Scripture—read 2 Peter 3:14–16

1 PETER / 2 PETER

The letters from

John

Who was John?

The writer of these letters is almost certainly the same as the writer of John's Gospel—the disciple whom Jesus loved. These might be the last of the New Testament writings. Since tradition tells us John finished his life in the city of Ephesus, they were probably written from that city around the end of the first century.

John seems to have been a very gentle and loving man. In his letters he constantly refers to the people he is writing to as his little children. This friendly form of speaking means he probably knew most of them, and so these letters were most likely written to members of the churches dotted around Ephesus.

Why did he write these three letters?

With the ever-improving abilities of everyday computers and printers, the counterfeiting of money is becoming an increasing problem. Recently there was a case of high school and college students working together to counterfeit hundreds of thousands of dollars. Don't even think about trying it, and especially don't ever say I gave you the idea!

Apparently the special agents who are trained to find counterfeit money are not given weeks of lectures on the great counterfeiters of the past, or shown all the best counterfeit notes ever produced. Instead, they spend all their time working with, looking at, feeling, and touching *real* currency. In the end, they know the real thing so well they almost have a sixth sense of what's counterfeit.

John, like Peter, wrote his letters to counter false teaching. Instead of spending a lot of time talking about what the false teachers were saying, he chose to write down the truth for his readers. He hoped they would come to know the truth so well that when false, or counterfeit, teaching came along, they would instantly recognize it for what it was.

sandwich full of cheesy goodness

sandwich made with nondairy cheese-food

1 John

It seems that when men and women grow old, they have two options: they can either become soft and sentimental, or they can grow really hard and bitter. I hope for your sake that your grandparents are of the former type. John certainly was.

For John, the key word is always love. He talks of the love God has for all of us, his children, and also of the love Christians should have for one another.

He then gives three ways you can know a true Christian—as opposed to a counterfeit one. True Christians will love other Christians, they will live righteously, and they will agree that Jesus was really man and God.

Interesting bits

We are God's children—read 1 John 3:1–10

Love comes from God—read 1 John 4:7–21

2 and 3 John

These two letters are both very short and very personal.

2 John is addressed to "the chosen lady and her children." This is probably not a real single-parent family but is another way of referring to a church (the chosen lady) and the members (her children). John encourages the church to go on growing in love, but not to be naive. The members are not to welcome people who do not teach the truth into their homes.

3 John is written to a particular church leader. When you read it, you can almost imagine it's a modern letter. John commends his friend on all the good he is doing but warns him against a particular church leader who is up to no good.

Interesting bits

There are only 27 verses altogether. Just read them, for goodness' sake!

The letter from

Jude

Some people are such name-droppers. They manage to bring their famous acquaintances into any conversation. "Thanks for the tea. Oh, that reminds me—did I tell you I once had tea with the Queen?"

Jude was not a name-dropper, though he could have dropped a bigger name than most. He calls

meet my half brother

half sister

quarter chicken

himself a brother of James and a servant of Jesus Christ. The James he mentions is likely to be the leader of the church in Jerusalem, the writer of the

book of James, and the half brother of Jesus.

Since Jesus had another brother named Jude, it makes sense that he is the one who wrote this letter. Jude was just being modest by not mentioning the fact he was Jesus' brother as well as his servant!

Why did he write this letter?

Well-organized people have their business categorized into jobs that have to be done today, this week, this month, and so on. I seem to work more along the lines of things I should have done yesterday, things I should have done last week, things I should have done last month, and back through time.

It seems Jude had been intending to write a proper, longer book, but the situation became so bad he had to get this one off the end of his quill and into the mail as quickly as possible.

Main theme

Once again the subject is false teachers. Rather than talking a lot about what they were actually teaching, Jude chooses to focus on the fate that awaits them—the terrible judgment of God. Thinking about that should be enough to keep sensible Christians well clear of them.

Interesting bits

A wonderful prayer of hope for all of us—read Jude verses 24–25

The Four Gospels

Matthew Mark	Acts	Romans 1 Corinthia
Luke John		2 Corinthians Galati
		Philippians Colossi
		2 Thessalonians 1
		2 Timothy Titus

The Acts of the Apostles

Paul's Letters

Other Letters

Ephesians
1 Thessalonians
Timothy
Philemon

Hebrews **James**
1 Peter 2 Peter
1 John 2 John 3 John
Jude

Revelation

Revelation

The book of

Revelation

Like all the best shows, the Bible goes out with a bang. No book is as exciting, as dramatic, or as confusing as the final one.

Who wrote it?

The book of Revelation was written by the Apostle John, who also wrote John's Gospel and the three letters of John.

Where and when did he write it?

Nobody likes his prisoners to escape—it just completely defeats the point. One popular trick has been to send the prisoners to a small island like Alcatraz or Patmos. Patmos?

Patmos was where the Romans sent political prisoners. John was there because of his Christian faith, but he managed to escape. Not literally—through a tunnel, or by taking a long swim—but through a series of visions that took him from the rocky little island up into heaven. There he was fortunate enough to be given a guided tour by Jesus himself.

The book of Revelation is the record of the visions or revelations—revelation, get it? The book was probably written around the middle of the last decade of the first century A.D.

Who was it written for?

The second and third chapters of Revelation give prophecies to seven churches in the Roman province of Asia. They were probably the first, but not the last, people to receive the written form of John's visions.

Why was it written?

If you were to tell friends that you worshiped the President, they would assume you admired his politics. If you tried again and explained that actually you worshiped him as your god, they would think your elevator didn't go all the way to the top floor.

In Roman times, the belief that the emperor was god was widespread. When Revelation was written, the sitting emperor actually required that everyone worship him. This got the Christians into a lot of hot water because they refused to worship anyone other than Jesus.

Christians in a lot of hot water

John wrote his visions into a book because he believed they would bring comfort and hope to persecuted Christians.

Main themes

Understanding Revelation

If your family has ever bought a new TV or video, you know that people have their own theories about what the instruction manual means. Even your two-year-old sister has an opinion—you have to lick it, wipe your nose on it, and tear it into little pieces before you can really understand it.

Revelation is about as simple to understand as an electronics instruction manual originated in Korean and translated to Japanese before making its way to English—which is to say, not very! There are many very different ideas as to how John's Revelation is best understood. Does it describe events already past or still to come? Or is it just poetic language that doesn't relate to specific real-world events at all?

If you're interested, you'll have to find your own answers to those questions.

Cartoons and caricatures

Name your favorite comic strip. Is it "Garfield"? "The Far Side"? Or the old favorite, "Peanuts"? Cartoons are a special kind of writing that we understand even though it's not always very linear. We know how to make sense of cartoons—how to uncover the joke.

STRANGE CREATURES

my friends Chris and Matt

bug-eyed monster

REVELATION

The book of Revelation is also a special type of writing, one the people John was writing to would have understood. It was called apocalyptic writing. Like our modern cartoons, it often used impossible or strange creations or caricatures of real people rather than straightforward descriptions. In part, this was a sort of code, and in part, it just made the book more dramatic.

Although Revelation can be hard for us to understand, there are some themes everyone will agree on.

To the churches

Few situations are as embarrassing as times when you believe you're alone, only to find you're not. Maybe you've got three fingers and both thumbs up one nostril, chasing the big one, and the boy you have a crush on walks around the corner. Or you're flashing your most macho smile to your own reflection in a window, and as your focus shifts you suddenly realize the teachers on the other side of the glass are laughing at you.

The seven churches of Asia probably had no idea how close a watch was being kept on them from above. When John sent them this little report card

from Jesus with their successes, failures, and areas for improvement all written down, I bet they decided to clean up their acts.

I know what happens!

Some TV shows can be watched again and again. But not detective stories. If you know who did it, and why and how, there's not much excitement in following Columbo and his raincoat around Los Angeles. You might as well go and visit the wrinklies at the nearest old folks home—a gesture for which you'd get lots of brownie points as long as you didn't admit you only did it because there was nothing on television.

However, in real life there are times when knowing how it's all going to turn out would be very welcome and save us a lot of worry and sweat. "Will she say yes, or won't she?" "Have I passed or failed?" "Will Mick Jagger ever take off those ridiculous wax lips or not?" And so on.

God gave John the revelations he did because the persecuted Christians of the early church needed to know that however bad things seemed, it was going to be all right in the end. So, in the middle of all the weird and wonderful creatures, pictures, and stories in the book of Revelation is a very simple message: God's in control, and we win!

Description of Jesus in heaven—read Revelation 1:12–18

The messages to the seven churches—read Revelation 2:1–3:22

The great crowd worships at God's throne—read Revelation 7:9–17

The white rider, Jesus, leads his army—read Revelation 19:11–21

Description of the new heaven and earth—read Revelation 21:1–22:21

letters to the seven churches

REVELATION

Don't look at me! Look at him!

Sounds like someone who's been caught doing something suspicious, doesn't it? He's standing there uncomfortably, looking extremely guilty, and he's desperately trying to shift the blame by pointing to someone else.

Well, for one thing it's rude to point—but that's exactly what I'm trying to do with this book. Let me explain.

Every author dreams of having a best seller. Imagine, being up there in the top 10 with the new John Grisham blockbuster, the revealing memoirs of an aging politician, and a book of exotic recipes from the TV chef du jour. Interviews on television, invitations to top literary lunches, and Steven Spielberg knocking on the door, begging to turn this masterpiece into a Hollywood hit.

Sounds great, and maybe one day it'll happen. But not with this book! You see, I'd be more than happy if you forget this book once you've read it.

"What did you say?"

Yes, that's right. The only reason this book has been written is to point you to another book, a much, much better book—*the* book.

Once you've put this book down, you might say: "Hmm, that was good. I laughed a little, learned a lot. Yes, I enjoyed that. Now I can start on that mystery novel." But that would be the wrong thing to say!

Yes, of course, read that mystery novel. But if this book hasn't made you want to go to the Bible as well, then I've failed miserably and I might as well have spent my days watching "Gilligan's Island."

Come on, dig into the Bible. It's exciting, challenging, life-changing. And you'll find the Bible is a book that points as well. It points to a person—a powerful and loving person, who has a plan for the human race and wants us to be part of it.

Now, I wonder who that person could be. Any ideas?

Hey, don't look at me! Look at him!

New Testament books in alphabetical order